practical
teaching skills for
DRIVING
INSTRUCTORS

4th edition

practical
teaching skills for
DRIVING
INSTRUCTORS

a training manual for the ADI
examination & the Check Test

john miller, tony scriven
& margaret stacey

Register of
Approved Driving
Instructors
(car)

**KOGAN
PAGE**

First published 1993
Reprinted 1994
Second Edition 1995
Reprinted 1996, 1997
Reprinted with revisions 1998
Reprinted 1999
Third Edition 2000
Reprinted 2001
Fourth Edition 2002
Reprinted 2003

Kogan Page Limited
120 Pentonville Road
London N1 9JN
UK
www.kogan-page.co.uk

British Library Cataloguing in Publication Data

A CIP record for this book is available from the British Library

ISBN 0 7494 3872 X

Typeset by Jean Cussons Typesetting, Diss, Norfolk
Printed and bound in Great Britain by Biddles Ltd, *www.biddles.co.uk*

Contents

Foreword

There are ever increasing demands on driving instructors, both in terms of the standard of instruction they are required to demonstrate and the need to meet customer aspirations, which require quality tuition to be given at all times. *Practical Teaching Skills for Driving Instructors* gives an insight into how to develop your teaching skills whilst preparing for the examinations, and how to improve on them in order to make your tuition more effective and enjoyable once fully qualified.

Qualifying as an Approved Driving Instructor is only the beginning of a satisfying and rewarding career. In a world of continuous changes it is essential that you strive to keep yourself up to date and improve on your knowledge, driving skills and teaching methods so that you are able to continue teaching 'Safe Driving for Life'.

Whilst I accept that during a Check Test the supervising examiner will only see a snapshot of your ability, those obtaining a Grade 4 or below should find something in this book to help them improve their teaching skills in order to achieve the highest grade possible. I would also hope that those ADIs gaining a Grade 5 or 6 work to the same standards when instructing during normal lessons. There is evidence to support the fact that the higher grade instructors present candidates for the driving test who are better prepared.

Practical Teaching Skills for Driving Instructors contains all the information you need to know on how to improve your teaching skills in line with current practices and established criteria. Putting into practice these skills should improve your teaching style and give you greater consistency in the work that you do.

Ian Taylor, ADI Registrar
August 2002

About the authors

The authors of *Practical Teaching Skills for Driving Instructors* all have over 25 years' experience in the driver training industry. This book was written by them in response to requests from numerous ADIs for a book that sets out, in simple terms, the good teaching practices needed to produce safe and effective drivers.

John Miller ran his own driving school in West Sussex for many years and is now an LGV training consultant with Millers Transport Training (part of the Page Group). He is a qualified tutor of driving instructors and co-author, with Margaret Stacey, of the DSA recommended book *The Driving Instructor's Handbook* (also published by Kogan Page).

Tony Scriven was involved in the formation of ADITE – The Approved Driving Instructors' Training Establishment directory (now ORDIT) – and served on its Committee for several years.

Margaret Stacey also served on the Management Committee of ADITE and then ORDIT as the representative of The Approved Driving Instructors' National Joint Council. She was a secretary to the Steering Committee that formulated the standards for the NVQ in Driving Instruction. Margaret is the author of *Learn to Drive in 10 Easy Stages*, *The Advanced Driver's Handbook* and the *AUTODRIVA Instructor Home Study Programme*, which is used, on licence, by other training establishments throughout the UK.

Practical Teaching Skills is recommended by the Driving Standards Agency for candidates training for the ADI examinations and for registered instructors preparing for the Check Test.

This book is complementary to *The Driving Instructor's Handbook* – now in its 12th edition and also recommended by the DSA.

Every effort has been made to ensure that this book is as up to date as possible. However, continual changes take place to legislation and also within the driver training and testing industry. This means that some changes may have occurred since going to print. To keep yourselves completely up to date, we therefore recommend that you regularly refer to *Despatch* (the DSA's own publication for instructors) and that you join one of the major ADI associations.

John Miller
Tel: 01243 784268
E-mail: john.miller@cwcom.net

Tony Scriven
E-mail: caza.azul@oninet.pt

Margaret Stacey
Tel/Fax: 01332 874111
E-mail: mstacey@autodriva.freeserve.co.uk
Web site: www.autodriva.co.uk

Introduction

Driving instructors use a wide variety of *practical teaching skills* (PTS) in their everyday work with learner drivers. These skills will have been acquired and developed in many other areas of experience, for example:

- at school;
- in college;
- working in other jobs;
- as a parent; and
- in life generally.

These practical skills and techniques that have been transferred from previous situations are known as 'transferable personal skills'. This term is used to define the skills that are personal to us as individuals and are capable of being used in different situations. For example, a pedestrian who is about to cross a busy main road uses skills in judging the speed and distance of oncoming traffic.

These skills, when recognised and 'transferred' to the new environment of driving, become very useful in traffic situations, for example when:

- waiting to emerge from a junction; or
- crossing the path of approaching traffic.

The skills are similar, but the environment is different.

Another example might involve the use of bicycle gears – a combination of decision making together with the physical skill of hand and foot coordination. This type of skill can be directly transferred to the car-driving situation.

Using your PTS to ensure effective learning takes place

To be able to teach learner drivers to cope with the fast, complicated and potentially dangerous environment in which cars are driven, it is essential that we develop our individual transferable skills and our *practical teaching skills*. This will ensure that effective learning takes place.

Remember that as driving instructors we are probably the only teachers whose 'classrooms' are travelling at high speeds along busy roads. In this environment your control and effectiveness as an instructor is a vital factor in the safety of your pupil, yourself and other road users.

To survive (in a business sense) in what is becoming an increasingly competitive market, you need to work continually at improving your:

- practical teaching skills;
- instructor characteristics;
- fault identification and analysis skills; and
- business skills and expertise.

National Vocational Qualifications (NVQs) are now available in the driver training industry. These are designed to recognise and build on 'competencies', with the emphasis on practical training and experience rather than on theory or examinations. This book is designed to help:

- candidates preparing for the Approved Driving Instructor (ADI) exams;
- practising ADIs preparing for their Check Test;
- those gathering evidence for NVQs;
- those involved in driver training at all levels who want to become more effective teachers in their everyday work.

Introducing practical teaching skills

As a professional driving instructor you need to be able to persuade your learners to do whatever you wish them to do, in the way that you want them to do it. Most of the practical teaching skills (PTS) dealt with in this book are dependent on effective communication skills. Instructors who can communicate effectively are far more likely to succeed in transferring their own knowledge, understanding, skills and attitudes to their learners.

Driving a car is potentially the most dangerous thing that many people are likely to do in their lifetime. Knowledge of the *Highway Code* and the ability to drive with a high degree of expertise are not in themselves sufficient qualities to be able to teach somebody else how to drive. The number of parents and spouses who have been unsuccessful with their teaching bears witness to this fact!

As a 'Driving Standards Agency (DSA) Approved Driving Instructor (ADI)' you should be aiming to teach your pupils 'safe driving for life' and not just training them to pass the test. As part of the qualifying process you are required to demonstrate not only your knowledge and driving ability, but also your communication skills and instructional techniques.

Whether you are a potential or a qualified ADI, this book focuses on showing you how to improve your teaching and communication skills so that you are better equipped to teach 'safe driving for life'. It also covers the preparation required for all three parts of the ADI examination.

TRANSFERABLE SKILLS

PTS can be developed to help you interact with your pupils, building on existing transferable skills. Many of these skills are not only 'transferable' from one environment to another, but are also 'transferable' from instructor to pupil.

Being a successful driving instructor relies not only on the traditional inter-personal skills, but also on being able to:

- use and interpret body language;
- sell ideas and concepts;
- solve problems;
- identify, analyse and correct faults;
- make immediate decisions with safety in mind.

To become qualified as an instructor you need to have, and to use, all these qualities. You also need to acquire learning and study skills and a basic under-standing of role-play.

ADIs are required to be able to communicate with their pupils in a variety of ways to suit the perceived needs of each individual pupil. You will be involved with selling, whether it is 'selling' yourself or your services to potential pupils or 'selling' ideas and concepts to existing pupils.

All of these skills are included because they are the ones that you must master in order to be able to develop your career. This book will show you how to improve your effectiveness by developing these practical teaching skills.

As already indicated, PTS and other transferable personal skills are not necessarily developed overnight. If you want to improve and develop your skills, you need to consider regular training and refresher courses as well as to continually monitor your own performance and effectiveness (see Chapter 10).

The need to practise these skills while you are giving lessons is just as vital as driving practice is to your pupils. To be able to learn from each encounter with a new pupil and to structure a self-development programme you must have an understanding of how studying, learning and teaching can be made effective.

Even more important is your ability to continually develop your own trans-ferable personal skills and to assist your pupils in doing the same. As well as driving ability, the skills of decision making, prioritizing and problem solving are just as important to the learner and qualified driver as they are to you, the instructor.

TEACHING SKILLS

To drive safely on today's congested roads requires knowledge, understanding, skill and an attitude that shows not only courtesy and consideration for other road users, but also the ability to make allowances for the mistakes of others – a 'defensive' attitude.

The development of sound PTS will assist you in achieving the objective of teaching driving as a lifetime skill. Many of the skills outlined are just as important to the development of the learner as they are to that of the instructor. They are 'transferable' from one to the other.

It is rather like preparing for the ADI Part 2 (own driving) examination.

> *The first person you have to teach how to drive is yourself.*
>
> *If you cannot achieve the right standard in your own driving, how can you possibly expect to be able to teach others how to drive properly?*

The same principle applies to skills other than driving. If you cannot master the skills of risk assessment, problem solving and decision making yourself, how can you expect to be able to teach pupils how to master them?

In an effort to improve the standards of L-driver training and driving instruction skills generally, the DSA have introduced various measures, including:

- the recommended syllabus for learner drivers;
- a 'Learners Log Book'; and
- 'Pass Plus' for newly qualified drivers.

You should take advantage of, and use, all of these initiatives, as they are useful in structuring your training and each pupil's learning.

Unfortunately, with the performance-based driving test system and the limited amount of time and money that the general public are willing to pay for lessons, ADIs are tempted to teach people how to pass the test instead of teaching them how to drive safely for life.

For similar reasons, the same applies to the ADI qualifying examinations: candidates are often trained simply to 'pass the test'. The practical teaching skills outlined in this book will equip you as an instructor or as a trainer to teach driving as a life skill, but the main responsibility for doing so lies solely with you.

The DSA's check test system, which has been upgraded over the past few years, has shown many experienced ADIs to be inarticulate, lacking in initiative and often unable to provide an effective learning environment for their pupils. Many have been found to be reluctant to accept criticism; others were unable to recognize and identify their pupils' basic driving faults – some of which were repetitive and serious.

DEVELOPING PRACTICAL TEACHING SKILLS

The skills covered in this book are highly transferable and should be of value to all ADIs who are concerned with improving their interpersonal effectiveness and about improving the skills of their learners. They should be adopted by:

- qualified instructors wishing to improve their career prospects;
- qualified ADIs and new entrants to the profession seeking employment – prospective employers will identify those who are best able to apply effective teaching techniques;
- all those who simply wish to improve, to become more self-confident and to influence their peers;
- ADIs preparing for their 'Test of Continued Ability and Fitness' (the Check Test) will find that improved communication skills and PTS will give them greater confidence and a better chance of achieving a higher grade;
- instructors preparing for the ADI qualifying examinations – particularly Part 1 (theory) and Part 3 (instructional ability). A better understanding of the skills required when teaching people to drive is an important part of these exams;
- tutors of driving instructors and staff instructors at instructor training establishments.

Developing the skills contained in this book is essential at this level of training; it is also totally compatible with the criteria for approval for the Official Register of Driving Instructor Training (ORDIT).

But there is no real substitute for practical, hands-on training and practice. You cannot learn how to drive from a book; neither can you learn how to teach someone from a book: the best way to learn how to teach is to teach!

EFFECTIVE LEARNING

The development of PTS is a continuous and lifetime process, with each new encounter offering you the opportunity to improve your skills.

Learning occurs in a variety of ways; however, as in most things, a systematic approach is invariably more effective than one that is haphazard. Trial and error in using skills will give some insight into the ones that are the most effective in different situations and with different types of pupil.

> *Reflecting on your successes and failures will also assist you in developing your practical teaching skills.*

Formal training and structured learning, both in-class and in-car, is invaluable to instructors wishing to develop their own skills. This applies even more when developing the more active learning strategies, such as role-playing exercises and fault assessment skills. Formal training for the ADI test allows you to practise new skills in a safe and controlled setting before trying them out on learners or trainees in the real world.

Experience gained while watching and listening to demonstrations given by your tutor will be valuable when you have to demonstrate skills to your pupils.

Training should be a continuous circle of learning:

- trainees learn from their tutors;
- pupils learn from their instructors;
- instructors learn from their pupils;
- information feeds back to the tutors;
- and so on...

The challenge for you is to adopt a frame of mind that welcomes each learning strategy, particularly those that require a more active approach.

> *The key element in teaching others how to drive (and in learning how to drive) is controlled practice.*

When teaching your pupils how to drive you should take every opportunity that arises to practise the skills contained in this book. Some skills training, however, can be seen to be slightly threatening to both learners and instructors. If care is not taken, embarrassment and offence can be caused when analysing someone's behaviour. Because of this factor, teaching a practical skill has to be delivered in a sensitive way. You should accept this fact from the outset. If you adopt too strict an approach, then your learners are unlikely to enjoy the experience and may feel reluctant to participate. Sensitivity must be shown to all your learners and this in itself is an important transferable skill.

Always remember that criticism can be very demotivating.

> *Encouragement when needed and praise when deserved will bring about more improvement than any amount of criticism.*

Chapter 2 explains how people learn. As a learner of PTS and transferable skills yourself, you must accept that training will not necessarily be easy and will demand a high degree of self-motivation and discipline. This is all part of your own learning process and will give you a better understanding of how your learners may feel when they are struggling to master new skills.

You will have to learn how to evaluate your own strengths and weaknesses, and will perhaps for the first time in your life, see yourself as others see you. This is also part of the learning process.

> *It is only when you see yourself as other people do that you can start to modify your own teaching skills. This will promote more efficient learning through the establishment of effective relationship skills.*

Never forget that there is no such thing as a bad learner. You must remember that some merely find it more difficult to pick things up than others.

To bring out the best in pupils the skill of the good teacher is in knowing when to:

- explain;
- demonstrate;
- repeat;
- assess;
- question;
- praise;
- encourage.

Being able to carry out all of the foregoing skills will enhance your teaching and ensure that more effective learning takes place. As you will be eventually sharing the road with your learners, this should be the main purpose of your job.

Just as your learners need to learn from any mistakes they may make during a driving lesson, you need to learn from your own instructional mistakes or weaknesses that may have led to that error.

At the end of each driving lesson you should ask yourself:

- How much *effective* learning has taken place?
- Could I have done any more to help my pupil achieve the objectives that we set at the start of the lesson?

Only by continually evaluating your own performance will you be able to improve and develop your PTS.

By using this book in a practical manner you can learn how to improve your PTS. This will benefit your pupils, help you to ensure success in the ADI examination, and help you to achieve the best possible grading on your Check Test.

Remember that learning is a continuous process!

Learning to drive

To help you develop or improve your practical teaching skills (PTS), it will be useful for you to understand:

- Why people learn to drive.
- What motivates them to learn.
- How learning takes place.
- What can cause barriers to learning.

THE BENEFITS OF LEARNING TO DRIVE

People learn to drive for a variety of reasons, but it is doubtful whether they ever fully realise the benefits of it until they have passed the driving test and become mobile. Think of some of your friends who drive and try to imagine how drastically their lives would change if they were to lose their licence.

When your pupils begin learning to drive they may be doing so for any of the following reasons:

- social, domestic or leisure pursuits;
- business and employment reasons;
- personal satisfaction;
- the need for independent mobility.

Other learners may be trying to rebuild their confidence after an illness or perhaps the death of a partner; some may have time on their hands and think that learning to drive seems like a good idea, while others may wish to learn merely because most of their friends can drive.

Whatever their reasons, it is only after they have passed the test that your pupils will realise how the other benefits gained from being able to drive will improve their quality of life.

The main benefits are:

- greater freedom and mobility;
- improved confidence and status;
- better employment or promotion potential;
- increased earning power.

When you consider these benefits, and also take into consideration that a driving licence remains valid until the holder's 70th birthday, driving lessons should be seen as remarkably good value for money. These benefits should be outlined when you are selling lessons and can be a very effective way of justifying what you charge.

MOTIVATION FOR LEARNING TO DRIVE

The motivation for learning to drive usually involves all of the different factors, both personal and external to the pupil.

One of the strongest motivating influences is peoples' own desire to fulfil those ambitions on which they have set their mind. Quite often this need for achievement will be linked to either prestige or monetary gain.

If you understand some of the personal factors governing the motivation of each of your pupils, it should help you to structure their lessons in a way that will also help develop the external motivating factors.

Most adults are mostly concerned with the immediate benefits to be gained from learning to drive. They will therefore, in the main, be more concerned with passing the test than with acquiring an understanding that will equip them with 'safe driving for life'.

However, as a good instructor, it is your responsibility to equip your pupils for a lifetime of safe driving. You will need, therefore, to ensure that the theoretical content of your course includes an understanding of anticipation and hazard perception.

It can be very useful to know why pupils wish to learn to drive as it will enable you to use those reasons for motivational support.

For example, if a pupil is finding a particular manoeuvre difficult, or complains about how much the lessons are costing, you should be able to placate them by saying, for instance, 'think how much easier it is going to be for you to get the kids to school each day!'

Because of the cost involved in learning to drive, it is unusual to find learners who are not motivated to some degree. However, they do exist. For example, a husband who has lost his licence through drinking and driving may want his wife to learn so that he doesn't lose his social life. The wife may have no interest in driving at all and may therefore find it difficult to learn. Stressing the benefits mentioned previously may help overcome this lack of motivation.

HOW ADULTS LEARN

Learning can be described as nature's way of enabling us to adapt and survive in a fast-moving and complicated environment. The driving environment is faster and more complicated than most. Problem solving and decision making often have to be carried out without the time to think things through that is usually available in other situations.

Often, safety is in question. Poor assessment of a situation and a wrong decision could be disastrous not only for the decision maker but for any passengers or other road-users.

Teaching can be described as creating an environment in which learning takes place. As a professional instructor, your car is your classroom.

The professional driving instructor must accept four assumptions:

● Learning is 'a good thing' because it enriches people's lives.

● While learning is inevitable and takes place all the time, the quantity and quality of learning can be massively increased if it is done deliberately rather than left to chance.

● Learning is continuous – therefore, it makes sense for it never to cease.

● Shared learning is much easier to sustain than solo learning.

You could give someone the keys to a vehicle parked in the middle of a field and say, 'Teach yourself how to drive that car. I will be back in two hours to see how you are getting on.' Surprisingly, if you came back two hours later, that person would have gained by his or her own initiative some basic ability in driving. Of course, we are not suggesting that you adopt this method.

Learning is the acquiring, over time, of skills, knowledge, understanding and attitudes. Learning is changing your behaviour so that you are able to do something that you couldn't do before.

Gender, race, age and intelligence have only indirect effects on a person's ability to learn. Recent research suggests that males and females use different parts of their brain in different ways to arrive at the same answers to similar questions. In view of a fall in the number of under 25-year-olds and an increase in the number of people in the 25–54 age group, it is likely that a greater proportion of older people will present themselves for driving lessons. Their training needs will probably vary from those of younger people.

Individuals' characters and family backgrounds are more likely to influence the way in which they learn than their age or gender alone.

In a structured learning programme, such as a course of driving lessons, both the pupil and the instructor should be able to see and measure any change in behaviour. This should allow both parties to decide how successfully learning has taken place.

Learning takes place in a sequence involving three interrelated stages. This is known as *the learning circle*.

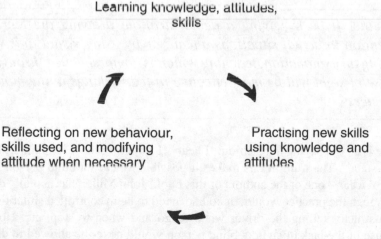

Learning knowledge, attitudes, skills

Reflecting on new behaviour, skills used, and modifying attitude when necessary

Practising new skills using knowledge and attitudes

The Learning Circle

Adults learn mainly through their senses, which provide them with information about the environment around them. These senses are personal to the individual and any two learners receiving the same information from their senses in a given situation, may PERCEIVE things differently. For example, one learner driver meeting oncoming traffic might perceive it as being potentially dangerous and decide to hold back. Another learner approaching a similar situation, might perceive no danger at all and go charging through the closing gap.

From the beginning, you should be aware that no two pupils are likely to react to a given situation in the same way. One of the golden rules of teaching is NEVER ASSUME.

Remember that in order to be able to teach a person how to drive, firstly you have to know all about driving, secondly you have to know about that person!

In learning to drive the three main senses used are sight, hearing and touch. However, other senses are sometimes used. For example, the sense of smell could make the driver aware that the engine is overheating or something is burning.

The importance of sight

In the learning process, sight is the most important of the senses. When teaching others to drive you can use this sense in a number of ways to improve the quality of the learning taking place.

Whether it be by giving a demonstration, drawing the learner's attention to actual situations ahead, or by using visual aids while giving an explanation, teaching which is comprehended through the sense of sight will be most effective in fixing things in the minds of learners.

There is an old saying in teaching: 'I hear – I forget; I see – I remember; I do – I understand'. The truth in this makes it possible to teach a blind person how to control a car – one of the authors of this book, John Miller, has actually done so – although the practice would, of course, need to be in controlled situations with the instructor telling the driver when to go and when to stop, etc. However, because of the lack of sight, a blind person would never be allowed to drive on the road!

The following diagram shows the proportions in which our senses gather information – our use of the diagram in this book itself testifies to the effectiveness of sight in the learning process.

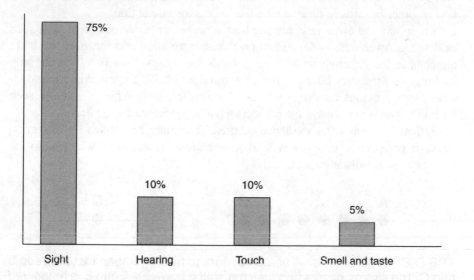

The proportions in which our senses gather information

If you told three learners in a classroom that 75 per cent of learning takes place through sight, with only 10 per cent occurring through touch, each of the students may have their idea of what 75 per cent looks like in relation to 10 per cent. By showing the visual aid, each pupil is able to picture the different proportions, thereby achieving a uniformity of perception which matches that of the students to that of the teacher.

The ability to persuade pupils to see and perceive things as the teacher does is a vital ingredient when teaching people how to drive.

As well as sight, hearing and touch play an important part and you need to ensure that when seeing situations, hearing the noise of the engine, and feeling the clutch coming to biting point, the learner not only develops all three senses but also the awareness and perception which go with them.

Awareness

In driving, awareness involves not only the perception and interpretation of one's own vehicle speed, position and direction of travel, but also the recognition of other hazards in time to take the necessary safe action.

Perception and awareness are the first steps towards performing a skill such as driving. Awareness is dependent on the interpretation and meaning the brain attaches to the information it receives from the senses. This involves not only looking with the eyes but also using the mind and calling upon existing knowledge from previous experience to 'see' with the mind. What is actually seen with the eyes is not always the same as what is perceived by the brain.

Optical illusions offer evidence of this. They may be caused by distortion through perspective or by a lack of intermediate visual keys which help the viewer to gauge distance accurately.

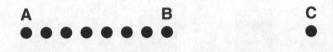

THE DISTANCE between A and B appears to be longer than that between B and C. The illusion occurs because the space between A and B is measured out in evenly spaced dots, filling the area for the eye. The distance between B and C can only be guessed at because there are no intermediate points.

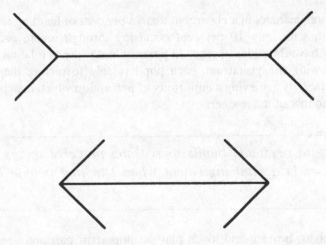

THE LENGTHS of the two horizontal lines appear unequal because of the directional arrows at the ends. Where the arrows branch outward, the line seems to be stretched out beyond its actual length. Where they branch in, the line seems to be strictly enclosed and shortened. Both of the lines are exactly the same length.

This visual distortion, plus a weakness in a driver's ability to judge correctly the width of the vehicle they are driving, or that of approaching vehicles, can have very serious consequences.

What each student actually perceives while learning not only depends on the individuality of their senses but on how that particular person has learnt to see and interpret things. You may need to modify the student's perception to make it compatible with your own as an expert on the subject.

Incoming sensations are instantly compared with existing knowledge stored in the memory from previous experiences. The compatibility of these memories can either help or hinder learning of any new material. Where the new information is compatible with existing knowledge and thoughts, the established memories will be reinforced. For example, somebody learning to play tennis who is already a good squash player may find the learning less difficult because both sports are very similar. This is called POSITIVE TRANSFER OF LEARNING.

Sometimes previous knowledge can be a hindrance to learning. An example of this could be someone who decides to learn to drive a car and has been used to riding a motorcycle in scrambling trials, an activity where success is dependent on the frequent taking of risks. Put this rider behind the wheel of a car on the road and the difference in the steering, the width and length of the vehicle and the differing speed norms required may all hinder the learning process. This is called NEGATIVE TRANSFER.

In this particular case, the learner is likely to be going for gaps which are too narrow, approaching hazards much too fast and struggling to master the steering at the same time.

TRANSFER OF LEARNING can also take place. This happens when a pupil uses skills which have been learnt in other environments to help in learning to drive. Examples include problem solving, decision making and prioritising, all of which form a part of everyday life in today's society. You will often be able to relate or transfer your pupil's existing skills to help in driving. However, where the new information is not compatible with established knowledge, it may be totally rejected.

It will take time for learners to establish the many thousands of memory connections needed to be able to drive safely, along with patience and understanding on your part. What you should try to do is make sure that the pupil 'sees' situations in the same way that you see them.

Other basic requirements which are necessary for learning to take place are:

- PERCEPTION;
- ATTENTION;
- ACTIVITY; and
- INVOLVEMENT.

The importance of perception

The senses vary from pupil to pupil and so does their perception. You will need to make your pupil's perception reasonably compatible with your own.

When you are driving along a wet road you will think that you 'see' a three-dimensional scene of slippery tarmac. What you *actually* see (the image in the eye) is neither slippery nor three-dimensional. This can only mean that you create in your mind a 'model' of what is there. You see the road as being 'wet' or 'slippery' because of the previous experience of such things you have 'fixed' in your mind.

A good example of this would be the lights of an oncoming vehicle on a dark country road at night. The amount of sensory information is very limited indeed but with your experience you should not have a problem interpreting it. You cannot see the vehicle but you know that it is there! You will build an image of the type and size of vehicle to which the lights belong and decide whether any defensive action is required.

Drawing on your own experience, you will need to help your pupils to 'fix' such things in their minds. This can be done by using question and answer routines regarding road surface, weather conditions, etc.

The diagram below gives an illustration of how the mind sometimes 'sees' things which may not be there in reality.

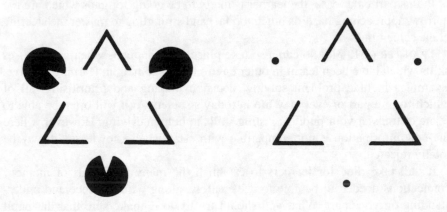

The central triangle in each of the figures is an illusion. Although we see the edges as sharp and clear, they are not there. There is no actual brightness difference across the edges; the triangle must therefore be constructed in the mind of the observer.

In the early stages of learning to drive some pupils will have difficulty in judging the width and length of the car they are driving, and the speed, distance and size of oncoming traffic.

Optical illusion caused by irradiation

At night the problem for the inexperienced driver may be made worse by an optical illusion called IRRADIATION. This is a physiological phenomenon that occurs when the eye focuses on neighbouring bright and dark areas.

Although both squares are identical in size, the image of the white square will to most people appear larger. Light coloured cars can therefore, in some situations, appear to be larger and closer than dark coloured cars of identical size.

Because illusions of this nature could have dangerous repercussions for your pupils, you should encourage them to take some of their lessons at night so that you are there to give guidance and can help to resolve any problems which may occur.

> *Perception is not always under the complete control of the learner and occasionally the mind will wander off in an unrelated direction.*

Attention

It is often difficult to maintain pupils' attention without a break or change of activity. For this reason, most lessons in schools are of 50 minutes' duration only. Those instructors conducting intensive courses should take account of the concentration levels of each individual student and plan for changes of activity, coffee breaks, etc, in order not to OVERLOAD the learner.

> *If you do not have the attention of your pupil, learning is unlikely to take place.*

You should watch for non-verbal signals from the pupil which may indicate boredom, impatience or fatigue (see Chapter 3, Body Language).

Activity and involvement

One of the best ways of making sure that your pupils are attentive is to actively involve them in the learning experience. Try to avoid very long briefings or explanations with no periods of physical involvement.

Activity, however, should not only be thought of as physical. Learning to drive obviously involves a lot of physical activity but it is often the mental involvement which initiates the physical response to a situation. The more active and involved novices are in the learning experience, the more they will normally remember. This is why PUPIL CENTRED LEARNING is so vital when teaching someone how to drive. The good instructor will help learners to think and reason things out for themselves, leading them to the desired conclusion.

Although you can use questions to test pupils' understanding of what they should be doing and why it is important, it is through physically carrying out the task that most learning will take place. This 'doing' VALIDATES the teaching and can be done in various ways. There are several different teaching methods that are commonly used by instructors:

Method 1 allows the passing on of information or facts with little intellectual activity on the part of the learner. Typical examples of this style of instruction are:

- teaching the answers to questions without confirming the pupil's understanding of the reasoning behind them; or
- telling the pupil to 'Always look round before moving off' without explaining why or finding out if the pupil knows what he or she is looking for.

Although this teaching method is limited it can be useful, especially in the early stages, provided your learners make use of the knowledge gained during their driving practice.

Method 2 involves asking a series of step-by-step questions that are designed to lead the learner towards the solution of a problem or statement of principle.

Open-ended or pointed questions which encourage active and creative participation, insight and contemplation, will bring about better understanding by the pupil than closed questions which only require a 'Yes' or 'No' response. When teaching a learner how to turn right you might ask:

'What is the first thing you would do before turning right?'

'Well, I would give a signal.'

'Wouldn't you do anything before that?'

'Oh yes, I would check my mirror.'

'Why is that important?'

'Well, I suppose there could be a motorcyclist overtaking me.'

'That's correct. And what would he be likely to do if you suddenly put on your signal as he was about to overtake you?'

'Well, he might suddenly brake or swerve around me.'

'Yes – so you would have caused him inconvenience or possible danger, wouldn't you?'

'Yes, I suppose so.'

'That's good. So, now you know why the "Mirror–Signal–Manoeuvre" routine is so important don't you?'

Because these open-ended questions are so important they are dealt with in more detail in Chapter 4.

Letting the learner explain correct procedures to you, the teacher, can be a very effective way of bringing about learning.

Method 3 is more 'PUPIL-CENTRED' than 'INSTRUCTOR-CENTRED' because it involves a higher level of participation from your learners, with them having to accept more responsibility for their learning.

Some aspects of driving instruction lend themselves to this 'pupil-centred' approach. For example:

- learning the rules in the *Highway Code*;
- learning about basic car maintenance from a book; or
- memorising basic driving procedures such as MSM, PSL or LAD.

Pupil-centred activities are quite useful when teaching in small groups where the instructor should act as a catalyst by:

- providing the necessary resources; and
- setting tasks for the learners to involve themselves in.

All knowledge gained through such activities must be transferable to driving practice. You will need to check that your pupils fully understand all the safety implications of practically applying the knowledge they have gained. This will also apply to the setting of homework and in-between lesson tasks which will need to be validated during practical sessions.

LEARNING WITH FRIENDS AND RELATIVES

Although some people still learn to drive with friends or relatives it has been shown that more than 95 per cent of all learners taking the Driving Test have had some professional instruction.

It may be that they have their initial instruction with a professional in order to acquire the basic skills required to control the vehicle or, more commonly, they acquire the basic skills with a friend or relative and then come to the professional just before the 'L' test saying, 'I just want to make sure I'm doing everything right!'.

Of course, in the latter case it is rather like 'shutting the stable door after the horse has bolted'. It is in this sort of situation that you will have a selling job to do. This may be in the form of selling more lessons, if there is enough time and money available, or selling the idea of postponing the test in order to give the pupil more time to improve and practise the correct procedures.

Unless the friend or relative carrying out the teaching has some form of instructional background, and is a reasonably good driver, it is a distinct disadvantage if the learner has received no lessons at all from a professional instructor.

Most friends or relatives tend to use trial and error methods, and the whole process can end up becoming unpleasant for both learner and teacher. It is also common for the person teaching to be out of date on traffic law, driving techniques and the requirements of the 'L' test. Otherwise there can be a 'negative' transfer of learning. As in most training, a structured approach is usually much more effective in helping the learners to achieve their objectives.

STRUCTURED TRAINING AND PRACTICE

The benefits of learning with a professional instructor should be:

- a better rapport between teacher and pupil;
- a saving in time and trouble;
- a higher level of knowledge, understanding, attitude and skill; and
- a better chance of passing the 'L' test and accomplishing safe driving for life.

To achieve the above objectives the professional driving instructor needs an understanding of how adults learn. Only through this understanding will the instructor be able to structure a programme of learning to suit the individual needs of each pupil (see Chapter 4, Teaching by Objectives).

One of the most effective methods of instruction is to use educational or instructional BEHAVIOURAL OBJECTIVES. Although there are no hard and fast rules, three main categories of learning have been identified as a basis for deciding the mode of instruction.

1. Behavioural objectives concerned with information and knowledge. This category covers the various mental processes – such as sensation, perception and thinking – by which knowledge is gained. This type of learning will usually involve using conventional issues and formally planned instruction.

2. Objectives that relate to the feelings, attitudes, emotions and values of the trainee. The following sequence shows the usual development of affective characteristics:

    (i) Learner/trainee becomes aware of feelings about a particular event/activity/topic.

    (ii) Learner/trainee conforms to instructions given by instructor/trainer regarding how he should feel about the particular event/activity/topic.

    (iii) Learner/trainee becomes capable of making value judgements on his own according to codes of conduct and principles now firmly established in his mind.

At the lowest level, the role of the learner/trainee is passive and limited to taking in information rather like a sponge with little personal concern. At the highest level, they will be integrating concepts, feelings and values into their own life/world.

You should help your learners/trainees to develop their feelings and values so that they end up with desirable attitudes. In particular, consideration for all other road-users needs to be fostered, especially for the more vulnerable groups such as children, old people, invalids, cyclists, etc.

3. This category is concerned with the learning of muscular and motor skills, such as co-ordination of the foot and hand controls, steering, etc. At the lowest level, behaviour will be clumsy and hesitant with frequent errors. After following a well-designed training programme, and with practice, complete mastery should be achieved. The pupil should be able to drive to a reasonable standard without assistance from the instructor. The skilled performance will be efficient and flow smoothly, with only minor errors being made.

During your normal working day you will find that your lessons involve using a combination of all three types of learning.

When taking a structured training course with a professional instructor, learning should be the result of a deliberate and directed effort. The learning plan should include:

● learning to memorise things;
● learning to understand things;
● learning how to do things;
● attitude development;
● developing study skills.

These elements are covered in the following sections.

Learning to memorise things

This is sometimes called ROTE LEARNING or PARROT-FASHION LEARNING and is the method by which most of us learnt our tables at school. Rote learning is rather limited in that it does not necessarily prove an understanding of the subject.

For example, a learner could memorise the overall stopping distances of a vehicle and be able to tell you, 'The stopping distance if you are travelling at 30 miles per hour on a dry road would be 23 metres'. The learner should then be asked to point out something that is 23 metres away!

Even when pupils can do this reasonably accurately, it is still necessary to test their ability to keep a safe distance from the car in front when driving at 30 miles per hour.

> *Knowledge in itself does not guarantee an UNDERSTANDING, nor the ability to use the knowledge and link it in with the skill of leaving sufficient distance between vehicles. Knowledge is often, therefore, just the starting point.*
>
> *The good instructor will need to use a skilful question and answer technique to verify understanding and test pupils' ability to put the knowledge into practice.*

This is sometimes known as VALIDATION: it involves proving that something has been understood by demonstrating the ability to carry it out.

Memory is vital for those learning to drive as it is no good learning something if two weeks, two years or 20 years later it has been forgotten.

The ability of your pupils to retain information and knowledge, and their capacity for forgetting what they have already learnt, will vary enormously from person to person. This is where the patience of a professional instructor will pay dividends as, with some pupils, there will be a need to explain things over and over again.

Up to the prime of life, the learning rate and the ability to retain information, knowledge and skills increase as the maturity level increases. After maturity both the learning rate and the ability to retain knowledge start to diminish.

Developing long-term memory

The first stage is to put the information in a form which can be more easily remembered by:

- breaking it down into its key components;
- using mnemonics – for example, MSM, PSL, LAD;
- painting pictures – 'What would happen if …?';
- using word associations like 'ease the clutch', 'squeeze the gas' and 'creep and peep'; and
- using visual keys – for example, 'round signs give orders, triangular signs give warnings', 'think of the thickness of a coin'.

When you have translated the information into a more memorable form, you could write it down and ask your pupils to memorise it by rote. You could then check whether they have remembered it by asking questions at the beginning of the next lesson. If they have not learnt it, do not lose heart. Explain to them that it is difficult to learn and encourage them to do some more studying.

Repetition is a very good way of fixing information in the brain, but care should be taken to ensure that your repetition does not sound like 'nagging'.

You should encourage your pupils to study the *Highway Code*, *The Official Driving Test* and *Driving – the essential skills*. You will then need to confirm that this has been done by testing their knowledge. You could set simple multiple-choice questions which could be given as homework, thus helping them both to maintain interest in between their driving lessons and to prepare for the theory test.

There are some very good videos available which you could loan to your pupils for home use. This should also help to maintain their interest. If you do this, however, you must ensure that you are not infringing any copyright restrictions.

Learning to understand something

An effective way of finding out whether your pupils understand something, is to ask them to explain it to you: '*why* do we have to look round over our shoulder before moving off'; '*what* must we do when we get to our turning point *before* we begin to reverse round the corner, and *why*?'

Understanding something means knowing its meaning, whether it be a statement of fact, a concept, or a principle. When a pupil is learning to do something, it is important that, to begin with, the key steps are understood, and then practice takes place until mastery has been achieved. ROTE LEARNING will be of little help to the pupil here and you need to use a technique that involves learning by understanding.

This method involves using mental processes as well as physical ones. It relies on the principle that the whole is greater than the sum of the parts. The easiest way to illustrate this is to use the analogy of a piece of music. Many of us often remember a catchy tune, to such an extent that we cannot get it out of our heads. It would be much more difficult, however, to remember just a few notes, and almost impossible to remember just one note, as this would depend on us having perfect pitch.

When teaching pupils how to approach junctions, you need to outline the complete manoeuvre and then break this down into its component parts. First of all, they need to understand the Mirror-Signal-Manoeuvre routine and then be able to break down the manoeuvre part into the Position-Speed-Look-Assess–Decide routine.

Not only do they need to understand the when, where, how, and why elements involved in these sequences, but they also need to practise carrying them out until a reasonable degree of safety is achieved.

No matter how well pupils understand and can carry out any component parts of the junction routine, unless they can approach and emerge safely, very little will have been achieved.

So the next teaching technique is to go back to whichever component part needs improving in order to get them to carry out the complete manoeuvre effectively. This may involve you in giving more explanation, possibly a demonstration and certainly more practice in order to improve performance.

All of these principles are dependent on the pupils' UNDERSTANDING.

> *There is little point in getting to the PRACTICE stage if pupils do not UNDERSTAND what is expected of them.*

The starting point in teaching understanding is to:

1. ask questions;
2. solve problems.

1. Asking questions

When giving information to learners, you should ask yourself, '*How, when, where, why* do we need to do that?' You will then need to ask the pupil the same questions, or give them the reasons. Good instructors will probably use a mixture of asking and telling in order to make lessons more varied. When using a question and answer routine, try not to make it sound like an INTERROGATION as this will only annoy or demoralise, and you may lose the pupil!

Try to relate any new information to what pupils already know (teaching from the known to the unknown). This will allow them to build up a store of understanding. It is of little use for your pupils to know how and when to do something if they do not understand *why* it is important.

We have all had pupils come to us from other instructors, or those who have been taught by friends or relatives, who are making mistakes and do not understand why what they are doing is wrong. For example, you may get pupils who signal every time they move off when there are no other road users in sight. When you ask, 'Why did you signal?' the reply is very often, 'My dad says you must always signal before you move off.'

It is obvious from this response that there is no understanding of what signals should be used for, nor how and when to use them.

> *Your job is to explain why it is important to assess each situation on its own merits, and then decide whether a signal is required or not. You could confirm this by asking, 'Who were you signalling to?'*

2.   *Solving problems*

You need to know how solving problems will help your pupils to UNDERSTAND things.

Solving problems usually relies on learners being able to transfer to new situations any knowledge and understanding already stored in their long-term memory. This should assist learners in working out different possible solutions to a particular problem.They can then evaluate these solutions and decide which is the most appropriate for the problem being dealt with.

> *To solve problems successfully, you will need to use intellectual skills to pose the appropriate questions, which will enable the correct solution to be arrived at.*
>
> *Once the problem has been solved, it is easier to understand why it occurred in the first place and how to prevent it in the future.*

The technique of problem solving is particularly useful when analysing the driving errors made by learners, whether they are in car (errors of control) or outside (errors of road procedure).

An example of this would be a learner driver turning left and swinging wide after the corner. The cause of the error might be obvious to the instructor, but not so obvious to the learner who may perceive several possible reasons for the error. Perhaps the steering was started too late, there was a misjudgement of the amount of lock needed, or the corner was approached at too high a speed, meaning that there was insufficient time to steer accurately enough to maintain the correct position.

> *Having recognised the fault, the good instructor would help the pupil to analyse the fault by using the question and answer technique to arrive at the cause of it.*

The first question could be: 'Why do you think you swung wide after the corner?' After a process of elimination, the pupil should eventually arrive at the correct answer.

Having solved the problem it would be necessary to take the pupil round the block in order to have another attempt at turning the same corner. You might choose to give the pupil a 'talk-through', particularly with regard to when to start braking and how much to brake, in order to ensure that the corner is negotiated more accurately. When success is achieved, the pupil should then be allowed to deal with similar corners unassisted, thus validating understanding and skill.

This all sounds fairly logical when you put it down on paper. However, it is sometimes surprising how some instructors would, first of all, fail to pinpoint accurately the cause of the error (not just the effect), and then not be able to assist the pupil in working out a solution to the problem, or to put the solution into practice.

Learning to do something (skill training)

In learning to drive, it is the practical application of the knowledge, under-standing and attitudes gained that is most important. Whatever the situation, when learning to do something there are three basic steps:

1. determine the purpose – WHAT and WHY;
2. identify the procedures involved – HOW;
3. practice the task – DO.

1.   Determine the purpose – WHAT and WHY

Learners must have a clear understanding of the reason for needing to be able to do whatever it is that you are teaching them. When teaching people how to drive the reasons why things are done in a certain way are invariably to do with:

- *Safety*
- *Convenience*
- *Efficiency*
- *Simplicity*
- *Economy*

One example that covers all of the above would involve the use of brakes to slow the car rather than the gears:

- *Safety:* Both hands are on the steering wheel when the weight of the car is thrown forward; the brake lights come on to warn following drivers.
- *Convenience:* There is less to do if you eliminate unnecessary gear changes.
- *Efficiency:* The car is being slowed by all four wheels rather than just two.
- *Simplicity:* It is easier to change gear at the lower speed.
- *Economy:* Brake pads and discs are much less expensive than clutches and gearboxes.

2.   Identify the procedures – HOW

The easiest way for the learner to understand how to do something is for the instructor to break the skill down into simple, manageable steps.

If it is a more complicated task, then the instructor should consider whether or not a DEMONSTRATION would benefit the pupil (see Chapter 4 – Explanation, Demonstration, Practice routine).

3.   Practise the task – DO

What I hear, I forget; What I see, I remember; What I do, I understand.

> *You must never forget that it is the doing that will give pupils the greatest UNDERSTANDING. In each driving lesson you must therefore give your pupil as much time as possible to PRACTISE the skills which have been learnt.*

The more time spent in practising the skill, the more improved the performance should be. As it is much more difficult to correct bad habits once they have become built in to the routines used by learners, good habits must always be encouraged.

Every instructor knows that it is much simpler to teach correct procedures to somebody with no driving experience than it is to correct the mistakes of somebody who has received poor instruction.

Although some car driving routines could be taught initially by ROTE (for example, the MSM, PSL and LAD routines), the application of them requires an *understanding* which then allows the pupil to make connections with any previously established principles.

For example, once your pupil has carried out one of the manoeuvres using the criteria of CONTROL, OBSERVATION and ACCURACY, it will then be relatively easy for them to follow the same pattern in similar but slightly more complicated manoeuvres – ie teaching from the known to the unknown.

As an instructor you will be mixing learning methods to suit the needs of each individual pupil, combined with the all important PRACTICE.

The skill of the teacher is to find a mix that works, or be prepared to change to a different mixture if necessary.

> *The key to good instruction is the flexibility of the instructor to be able to work out what is best for the pupil, and adapt the teaching to suit.*

Attitude development

Positively developing a driver's attitude is no different from developing the other transferable skills. You must have the correct attitude towards driving in order to be able to transfer a similar attitude to your learners.

You will need to develop your learners' assessment and decision-making skills so that they become compatible with your own. Remember, you must be able to persuade learners how to do what you want them to do, in the way that you want them to do it. For example, do your learners:

- show courtesy and consideration for other road-users at all times?;
- reduce the risk of accidents by planning well ahead?;
- follow the rules in the *Highway Code*, keeping within the law?;
- think defensively instead of aggressively?; and
- always consider the consequences of unsafe actions?

Encouraging the correct attitudes can sometimes be quite difficult to achieve, especially when teaching adults. Previous knowledge and learning can get in the way and old attitudes are difficult to modify.

The learner comes into this world with no attitudes about anything. Attitudes are formed early on, mainly by association with friends, relatives or groups with strong views on particular subjects. In the driving task, a learner who, for example, has spent a lot of time as a passenger alongside an aggressive experienced driver may regard this driver's behaviour as the norm and is likely to adopt a similar attitude. When the learner realises that this attitude is different from yours he or she may attempt to put on a show just for your benefit, or for the benefit of a driving test examiner.

Attitudes are formed from three constituents:

1. KNOWLEDGE
2. MOTIVATION
3. EMOTION

The attitudes of learners can be changed, through skilful persuasion, by modifying their views and the decisions they make in any given situation.

To assist in this modification of attitude, you could use accident statistics regarding new drivers, safe driving videos, the high cost of insurance for newly qualified drivers, the New Driver Act and the possibility of losing their licence, etc.

> *There is little doubt that attitudes have an enormous influence on the behaviour of the driver and the development of favourable attitudes is probably the most effective long-term method of reducing road accidents.*

By far the most useful aid to attitude development is the continual use of the DEFENSIVE DRIVING theme, pointing out the safety benefits to your pupils.

Defensive driving

You can contribute positively towards reducing the risk of accidents by teaching your pupils defensive driving techniques and attitudes. The development of a defensive attitude is probably more important than skill development. It is good to be able to get out of trouble when a potentially dangerous situation arises, but it is much more effective and clever to avoid getting into trouble in the first place!

The theory of defensive driving relies on research and statistics that show that human behaviour is generally motivated most powerfully by a desire to preserve one's own safety. Defensive driving develops this concept by instilling in drivers an attitude designed to do just that, coupled with the advanced observation of potential accident situations. It may be defined as 'driving in such a way as to prevent accidents, in spite of adverse conditions and the incorrect action of others'. The need for teaching defensive driving skills is emphasised by the DSA's introduction of 'hazard-perception' testing.

An accident has been described as 'an unforeseen and unexpected event', but in many cases potential road accidents *can* be foreseen and in most cases, when they happen, are caused by driver error. Everyone then asks who was to blame. Of far more value to driver education is to consider: 'Was it preventable?'

A preventable accident is one where a driver – not necessarily at fault – could reasonably have taken some action to prevent it happening.

The Driving Instructor's Handbook goes into more detail on hazard awareness, reducing risk and the theory of defensive driving. Some of the factors involved in road accidents are:

- visibility;
- weather conditions;
- road conditions;
- time of day;
- the vehicle; and
- the driver.

In this section we will be concentrating on the driver and how we can instill into our learners a 'defensive attitude'.

Human actions which may contribute to accident situations are:

- committing a traffic offence;
- abuse of the vehicle;
- impatience;
- sheer discourtesy; and
- lack of attention.

The defensive driver will consider all the factors in the first list, making a continuous and conscious effort to recognise each hazard in advance, understand the defensive attitude needed, and maintain the skill required to take preventive action in sufficient time.

You should encourage your pupils to drive with full concentration to avoid potential accidents caused by other drivers and road-users.

A constant awareness is required so that, no matter what they do, other road-users will be unlikely to be involved in an accident with drivers you have trained.

If another driver clearly wants priority, train your drivers to give way – better a mature decision than a lifetime of suffering as the result of an accident. Teach your pupils how to avoid confrontation and to keep a cushion of safe space around their vehicle at all times. This should include advice about a driver who follows too closely.

Get them to ask continually, 'What if...?' – in this way they will improve their anticipation skills and be able to take defensive action before a situation develops into an accident.

Teach them to consider using the horn to let others know they are there, just a gentle dab on the horn can sometimes prevent an accident. It is far better for your pupils to sound the horn to alert another person than not to sound it and have to carry out an emergency stop, especially if there is somebody else close behind.

As well as thinking defensively, favourable attitudes should be developed towards:

- vehicle maintenance and safety;

- traffic law (eg, safe use of speed, traffic signs and road markings, parking restrictions, drink/drive laws, dangerous driving implications);
- the more vulnerable groups of road-users;
- reduced-risk driving strategies;
- further education and training for advanced/defensive driving; and
- learning and studying.

Developing study skills

You will need to develop your study skills because your self-development programme is dependent on studying. However, driving is mainly practical so you will be studying, literally, while 'on the job'.

You may at some stage in the future wish to gain extra qualifications or take some remedial or specialist training – this will also involve you in studying.

Your learners too will need to study between lessons in order to prepare for the theory test. You will need to assist them in the studying and preparation process.

In developing study techniques one needs to:

- make time available;
- find the right place; and
- formulate a study plan.

Making time available

You will have to emphasise the importance of revising between lessons and explain to pupils why they may need to reorganise any social activities so that their studying is effective.

The key is to help them establish a balance between each demand on the time they have available. They should not be forced to devote all of their time and energy to studying at the expense of other interests and activities as this may cause resentment.

You may also have to consider the needs of your pupils' families. One of the best ways of achieving this is to get the family involved with the studying, perhaps by helping to test the student's knowledge, or looking through any written work which has been done.

Time management is crucial. Whenever possible, exploit those times of the day when the student is in the best frame of mind for studying, scheduling any other interests around them.

Initially, the student should try out different times until a routine is established which allows time for studying alongside other demands.

The key ingredients contributing to the success of any studying are self discipline and determination. Inability to sustain this motivation will make learning much less effective.

To reinforce this determination, the student should continually go through all the benefits that will be acquired after successfully completing the course of study.

Finding the right place

This is almost as important as making the time available. The quality of learning is improved dramatically if the environment is 'conducive to learning'.

Certain types of learning – for example memorising information – require a quiet environment, free from distractions. For most people a room at home which is quiet and respected by other family members as a study room will be the best setting.

There needs to be space available for books, etc, and a chair and table suitable for writing. Noise distractions should be kept to a minimum as they will reduce concentration and impede the learning process.

When a time and place for studying have been found, they should not be wasted. A structured approach to studying will give the best results.

Formulating a study plan

Studying is a skill which, like all skills, will improve with practice, determination and a planned approach.

Some people are naturally studious – they are content to spend hours at a time studying and reading. For others, studying requires effort. Other interests have to be shelved, distractions removed, and full concentration given to the task. To help in improving the quality of studying, students need a plan. For example the student should:

- set a personal objective and a time by which to achieve it;

- decide how much time each day/week will be needed to achieve the objective by the deadline set – students should be guided by other learners/ instructors/tutors as to how much time might be needed;

- prepare a formal study timetable for the duration of the learning programme, on which target dates for completing the component parts of the subject can be indicated;

- make sure the timetable includes relaxation time between study periods, with at least one whole free day per week and one or two study-free weeks if the programme is protracted;

- keep a continuous check on the progress made so as to adhere to the study timetable and not fall behind;

- not get dispirited if they fall behind but decide whether any leisure activity can be sacrificed to catch up with the study programme;

- not panic if pressures from studying build up, and discuss the pressure with friends, relatives, other students or instructors/tutors;

- consider lowering their targets and, perhaps, revise the timetable to extend the deadline if this is possible; and

- never let the study programme get on top of them, but keep on top of it!

BARRIERS TO LEARNING

As well as being aware that your pupils will learn at different rates, and that your training will need to be structured to take this into consideration, you need to know that some of them will experience *barriers to learning*.

These barriers may affect:

- learners' studies for their theory test;
- the rate at which they learn to drive the car; or
- a combination of both.

There are many barriers to learning that you will need to help your pupils overcome. As a general rule, the older the student, the greater the barriers tend to be.

Learning is the bringing about of more or less permanent changes in knowledge, understanding, skills and attitudes. Adults in general find that learning new skills and developing fresh attitudes is more difficult than gaining knowledge and understanding. Barriers to their learning may have to be overcome in any or all of these areas.

In adult learning the most frequently encountered barrier is *previous learning*.

Previous learning

Take the young man who has developed a partial sense of speed as a passenger, perhaps being driven by an aggressive young company car driver. He will have subconsciously formed an impression of speed norms gained while sitting next to his friend. This could be detrimental when the novice tries to emulate the experienced driver. Unless dealt with in a sensitive but firm and positive way by his instructor, this could not only seriously hinder the progress of the learner but may also be dangerous.

Take the learner who comes to you from another instructor who is less up to date than you are, or someone who has received some 'lessons' from an elderly relative who has been driving for 50 years. They may have been misinformed. For example, two widely held – but false – conceptions are that it is good driving practice to:

- always change down progressively through the gears when slowing down or stopping; and

- always signal when moving off, passing parked cars and parking whether it is necessary or not.

Where the novice has been influenced by old-fashioned views it is likely to become a barrier to learning and cause conflict with the new information given by you.

When this type of interference occurs, you must find ways of convincing the pupil that a change in ideas is necessary.

You will need to exercise considerable sensitivity, tolerance and patience during this period of unlearning.

One of the ways of overcoming the problem would be to show the pupil the 'official view' in *Driving – the essential skills*. This will add weight to your words and help to convince the pupil that change is necessary.

Another way would be for you to prepare a balance sheet, listing the benefits of carrying out the correct procedure (your method) and then asking the pupil to write down all the benefits of carrying it out their way.

Lack of motivation is also a barrier to learning. However, where driving instruction is concerned, because of the costs involved, this is not a common problem (as was stated in the section dealing with motivation for learning). You could, however, have some pupils who are not paying for lessons personally, such as those whose employer wishes them to pass the test in order to help with the firm's business activities. These people may have no desire at all to learn to drive.

To overcome this lack of motivation, you would need to outline the personal benefits of learning and also the consequences of not keeping the boss happy!

Other barriers to learning are:

- ILLITERACY;
- DYSLEXIA;
- COLOUR BLINDNESS;
- LANGUAGE DIFFICULTY;
- DEAFNESS; and
- PHYSICAL DISABILITY.

Illiteracy

Being unable to read and write can be a barrier to learning how to drive. However, if you are prepared to adapt your teaching to suit the needs of your pupil you will usually find ways of overcoming these problems.

Two-fifths of the world's population are deemed to be illiterate but, in Northern Europe, the incidence of illiteracy is extremely rare. Very often, people who cannot read or write make up for these inabilities by being very practical and dextrous and frequently pick up driving with little or no instruction at all!

You will need to use visual aids, discussion and demonstration to get your message across. It would also be useful to involve the pupil's family in assisting with study and learning. Help will be needed particularly with the *Highway Code* and other essential reading materials.

Dyslexia (word blindness)

The inability to recognise certain words or letters is called dyslexia. Neither its cause nor its effects are easily explained. Partially genetic, it can be described as a disorganisation of the language area of the brain which, in turn, produces problems connecting sounds with visual symbols.

The net result is more readily understood. A dyslexic may experience learning difficulties with reading, writing and mathematics. Ignorance of dyslexia in the past branded its sufferers as stupid when they were anything but.

Dyslexia is uncommon and, again, should not present a problem to the instructor who is prepared to vary the instruction to suit the needs of the pupil. Visual aids should be used and help given in recognising and acting on traffic signs.

More help may be needed when learning *Highway Code* rules and driving principles. You should also try to encourage the pupil's family to help with the study.

Interactive computer programs are now available to help people with dyslexia overcome some of the problems.

Colour blindness

This is likely to cause problems only when dealing with the different types of traffic light controlled situations such as junctions and pedestrian and level crossings.

Rather than focusing on the colours, you will need to base your explanation on the positioning and sequence of the lights and what each of them means.

Language difficulties

If pupils' understanding of English is very poor, this can be a barrier to learning and, in extreme cases, the learner might need the help of an interpreter.

Providing the pupil has some knowledge of English, the use of visual aids, demonstrations and getting to know what the limitations are, will help you to overcome these difficulties.

It is important, right from the start, for you to encourage pupils to say if there is anything they have not understood.

If there is someone in the family who speaks better English than the pupil, it may be useful to have a debriefing with them present. This should enable you to clarify specific requests to the pupil and also allow the pupil to convey any queries to you.

Teaching people who have hearing difficulties

This section gives guidelines that should help you to adapt the PTS in this book when teaching people with hearing problems.

There are about 50,000 people in the UK who were either born without any hearing or who lost it during early childhood. There are several thousand others who have become profoundly deaf in adult life, well after they have learned to speak, read and write. By the time they reach the age of 17 and are thinking about learning to drive, those with severe hearing problems may have had most of their education in specialist schools or units. Some will have speech, but this may be difficult to follow – especially for anyone who is not used to dealing with this type of disability. They will probably use sign language and may also be able to lip-read.

With understanding and patience from an effective instructor, people with hearing difficulties should be able to assimilate all that is necessary to learn to drive.

Although not being able to hear will undoubtedly be a barrier to learning, an understanding of the pupil's special problems will quickly enable you to overcome them.

People who cannot hear do not regard themselves as being disabled. Indeed, deafness is not classed as a driver disability so no restrictions are placed on the full licence.

It is particularly important for deaf people, and those with no useful hearing at all, to disclose this fact in the 'Disabilities and special circumstances' box in the DSA application form for the driving test (DL26). This will ensure that the examiner will be prepared to modify the method of delivery of instructions to suit the candidate's particular needs.

If the learner has neither hearing nor speech, he or she will be allowed a special interpreter.

When no interpreter is to be present, you must find time to talk to the examiner well before the date of the test so that you can explain which method has been used to give directions and instructions during training. The examiner can then give directions and instructions that are compatible. This will mean that the pupil on test is much more likely to be relaxed.

Unfortunately, instructors are not often asked to teach pupils who have hearing problems, and when asked are sometimes reluctant to do it. This is mainly because there is a widespread lack of understanding of the problems of people with hearing difficulties and the ways in which they are able to communicate . For many instructors the task may seem too daunting. As a result, people without hearing often find difficulty in obtaining expert tuition and tend to rely on parents and friends – people who may be good at communicating with deaf people but who are not necessarily able to teach safe driving for life. Driving instructors who are specialists in communication, have good PTS and who understand the effects of not being able to hear are better equipped to teach than friends and relatives.

After adapting your PTS to teach deaf people how to drive, you will find the experience both rewarding and enriching. The problem for you will be to learn the best way to transfer your knowledge, skills, understanding and attitude to these pupils.

PTS for teaching deaf people how to drive

It is not necessary for you to learn the British sign language used by deaf people, but you must use simple straightforward words which have only one meaning, avoiding those which may be ambiguous.

As lip-reading depends as much on the clarity of the speaker's lip movements as on the ability of the deaf person, it is essential that you speak slowly and distinctly, and move your lips to form each word. Face-to-face conversation while stationary becomes more important than with a hearing pupil. Never shout – the pupil cannot hear what you are saying!

With impaired hearing, sight and touch become a great deal sharper and this helps pupils to overcome the disadvantage of not being able to hear. They are likely to be much more aware of what is happening on the road ahead and will quickly master how to assess risk.

People without hearing also develop great sensitivity of feeling over the normal course of living in silence. Consequently, they often acquire clutch control and coordination with the accelerator fairly easily.

People with hearing problems normally have better powers of concentration than learners with normal hearing.

Pupils who cannot hear:

- do not lack intelligence;
- are eager to learn; and
- are less likely to forget something they have been taught.

Communication between you and pupils with any hearing difficulty, whether this be through the use of visual aids or signing, should be reinforced with demonstrations.

When teaching those with a hearing problem it is vital that a method of communication acceptable to both of you is established at the begining of their first lesson.

No matter what problems a pupil may have, the normal skill-training pattern of *Explanation – Demonstration – Practice* must be followed. However, because of the risk of any danger arising through misunderstanding, the *explanation* needs to be more thorough. You must ensure that learners with hearing problems fully understand the safety aspects of any driving skill before being allowed to practise it.

Pre-prepared cards which cover *what, how, when* and, most importantly, *why* can be used. The cards can be used to reinforce the KEY POINTS of any manoeuvre or exercise with drawings of pedestrians, cyclists and cars indicating the involvement of other road users. A magnetic board can be useful to recreate situations quickly and easily.

When giving directions, a simple form of sign language can be used provided you both agree and understand the signs to be used. These signs, because they are being used while the vehicle is moving along the road, will not be the same as those used in the British sign language. This must be explained to, and fully understood by, the pupil. For example, putting a thumb up will mean 'good', whereas putting a thumb down will mean 'incorrect'.

As a large amount of learning will take place through the eyes, it must be understood how the task of teaching deaf people becomes easier with the use of visual aids and demonstrations. Visual aids are not only invaluable, they are essential. (See Chapter 4 – The Use of Visual Aids).

Face-to-face conversation, simple language and written notes should cover all of the other needs of the deaf pupil.

Because you will not be able to use an effective question-and-answer technique while on the move, diagrams such as those in the *Autodriva Visual Teaching System* (published by Margaret Stacey – details in 'About the Authors') will be invaluable when teaching pupils with hearing difficulties. More time will need to be spent parked somewhere safe so that non-verbal instruction can take place.

A complete practical teaching booklet produced by the late Elwyn Reed MBE explains in detail a system for teaching deaf people how to drive. This is recommended to all those who are considering extending their PTS by undertaking this worthwhile activity. Details of the booklet, which has been approved by The British Deaf Association, are available from:

The Institute of Master Tutors of Driving
12 Queensway
Poynton
Cheshire SK12 1JG

Tel: (01625) 872708

The diagrams and illustrations in this booklet, together with your own visual aids and PTS, will be of great assistance in your work.

It is important to acquaint pupils with all the safety requirements of the L test outlined in the DSA publication *The Official Driving Test*. Ensure that they completely understand what is expected from them when carrying out the set manoeuvres, particularly regarding the observations to be made.

Learning the theory of driving for those with hearing difficulties

The DSA videos on the *Highway Code* and *The Official Theory Test* will be useful for pupils to study in between lessons. Questions can be devised in written form to test their understanding of the rules.

Always have a writing pad handy so that any questions and answers can be written down.

If any problems arise, you will benefit from talking to the parents or relatives of pupils and getting in touch with any local associations for deaf people or:

The British Deaf Association
1–3 Worship Street
London EC2A 2AB

Tel (020) 7588 3520

Physical disability

Physical disability need not be a bar to driving. There are thousands of people with disabilities, some quite severe, who have passed the Driving Test. Many have proved their skill by also passing an advanced test.

Teaching people with disabilities can be very rewarding as they usually have lots of motivation to learn and often put in more effort than their able-bodied peers.

If you do accept the challenge, the PTS in this book will help you to improve the quality of learning taking place. In particular, you will need to pay special attention to the following:

- *Flexibility* – being able to adapt your usual teaching methods to suit the perceived needs of the pupil.
- *Lesson planning* – being prepared to build in rest breaks and taking care not to spend too long on manoeuvres which may put physical strain on the pupil.
- *Body language* – watching carefully for signs of strain.
- *Feedback* – offering feedback only on things that are controllable. Telling a pupil he or she is not reversing properly because they are not turning round in the driving seat sufficiently is not very helpful if they are unable to turn any further owing to the disability. In this situation another solution must be found – for example, fitting extending side mirrors.

Fitting out a vehicle with lots of modifications to suit a wide variety of disabilities can be very cost prohibitive, unless you have a wide catchment area of prospective pupils. Sometimes an automatic vehicle may be all that is needed to overcome the problems of some disabilities.

Three fairly common disabilities which can be overcome relatively simply, enabling effective teaching are:

- having only one leg;

- having only one arm; and
- restriction of head, neck or body movement.

Someone with no left leg should be able to drive an ordinary automatic vehicle, while somebody with no right leg will be able to get pedal extensions/adaptions to enable the accelerator and brake of an ordinary automatic vehicle to be operated with the left one.

Someone with only one arm should also be able to drive an automatic vehicle with a steering-wheel spinner fitted. These can be fitted or removed in a matter of minutes.

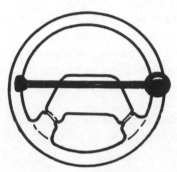

Steering-wheel spinner

There are number of different types of spinner to suit the individual needs of the person. See examples below:

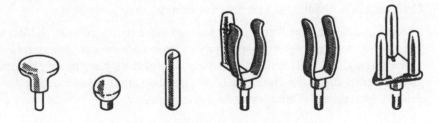

Different types of steering spinners

Using this type of adaptation means that a standard automatic transmission vehicle could be used by disabled people and the steering spinner easily removed for use with able-bodied pupils.

For those with restricted movement of the head, neck or body, special mirrors may be fitted to remove the need to look round before moving off or changing lanes.

Those people wishing to learn to drive who have quite severe disabilities should normally be advised to seek an assessment from specialists at one of the mobility centres around the country. A list of these is included in *The Driving Instructor's Handbook*. If it is considered that they will be able to learn successfully, they will be advised on how a suitable vehicle of their own could be adapted to help overcome their problems. Lessons will, in these cases, be conducted in the pupil's vehicle.

You may need to allow extra time at the beginning and end of lessons for the pupil to get in and out of the vehicle. Frequent breaks may be necessary during lessons if the pupil is prone to tiring easily or becomes uncomfortable after sitting in the same position for a while.

> *You will need to assess each pupil's personal requirements, and adapt your teaching methods to suit them.*

Some people tire very easily as the day progresses. Lessons should be arranged at appropriate times so that pupils will be 'at their best'. This will ensure that as much learning as possible takes place. You will need to find out pupils' weaknesses and strengths and work out the best ways of dealing with them so that problems are minimised.

If you wish to specialise in this kind of work, it is recommended that you attend a course for instructors in teaching people with disabilities. These are conducted at the Banstead Mobility Centre in Carshalton, Surrey (Tel: 020 8770 1151).

Other impairments

Mere discomfort can be a barrier to learning. You need to be able to recognise whether or not your pupils are comfortable. Discomfort can have many causes, ranging from toothache to sitting in an incorrect position, or being told, 'You must keep your heel on the floor when using the clutch' when the pupil's feet are too small or their legs too long to do this comfortably.

Allowances may have to be made for very tall people – they will need the seat as far back as possible with the back rake adjusted to give more leg room. If the tuition vehicle is very small, it may even be necessary for you to advise them to take lessons with another instructor who has a larger car with more headroom.

Pupils of small stature may be assisted by securing cushions underneath and behind them, and pedal extensions may be needed for those with short legs or small feet. Your terminology may also need to be adjusted to allow for pupils not being able to keep their heel down when controlling the clutch.

If a pupil is not driving as well as usual there may be some simple explanation. For example, was the driving seat adjusted properly on entering the vehicle, or was the pupil in too much of a hurry to 'get going'? Make sure these minor procedures are carried out correctly otherwise you may both be at a loss as to the cause of the problems and the lesson may be wasted.

If the pupil is having an uncharacteristically bad lesson, it may be due to something as simple as wearing different shoes, or as complicated as having problems at home.

Ask tactfully if you think a pupil may not be feeling well. The lesson may be completely wasted if a minor illness is causing a distraction. You could even be aiding and abetting an offence if the pupil is taking drugs which affect driving.

Others barriers to learning to drive can be caused by the use of alcohol which, as well as being illegal, can cause a false sense of confidence and impetuous risk-taking. If you think a pupil has been drinking, ask tactfully and abort the lesson if necessary. On no account do you let the pupil take the test if they have been drinking.

Anxiety, emotion and stress can all affect concentration. If a pupil's driving is not up to the usual standard and they have recently had personal problems, it may be advisable to postpone the lesson. Explain that it is not the best time to drive as they will not be able to concentrate on the road and traffic environment.

We are all affected by the ageing process. For those who decide to learn to drive later on in life the going can be difficult. You should explain that it will be more difficult to learn and to remember new procedures. Things may be more easily forgotten and concentration more difficult to sustain. Problems may be even greater for those in this age group who have decided to learn to drive because they have lost a partner or close relative. You will need lots of patience and understanding if you are to help these pupils attain their goal.

Continually assess your own effectiveness by asking yourself:

- Do I stress the benefits of learning to drive in order to motivate my pupils?

- Do I structure my teaching to make it easier for them to memorise, understand and do things?

- Do I pay enough attention to developing or modifying their attitude towards driving and other road users?

- Do I help them to develop their studying skills, setting them enough 'between-lesson tasks'?

- Do I help them to overcome any barriers to learning which they may have?

3

Communication skills

People learn all the time. If you did not learn you could not deal with the environment in which you live and work. You would constantly stub your toe on the foot of the bed, burn your fingers when cooking and press the wrong button when adjusting the television set.

Because the driving task is both difficult and potentially dangerous, driving instructors should accelerate the learning process for their pupils. You should ensure that you teach your pupils to understand the hazards and deal with them as soon as possible. In this chapter we will be concentrating on the essential Practical Teaching Skills (PTS) of communication which will help to bring about learning when teaching people to drive. These PTS include verbal, non-verbal and listening skills.

The Driving Standards Agency (DSA) considers that Approved Driving Instructors should be:

- ARTICULATE;
- ENTHUSIASTIC;
- ENCOURAGING;
- FRIENDLY;
- PATIENT; and
- CONFIDENT.

During the ADI Part 3 test of instructional ability and the periodic Check Test, these characteristics must be demonstrated and are assessed. Most of the

INSTRUCTOR CHARACTERISTICS will be displayed while the instructor is communicating with pupils during driving lessons.

SPEAKING SKILLS

As an instructor you must make sure that you use speech effectively and in such a way that your pupils will hear and understand what it is that you need them to hear. For example, even though you may be frustrated or exasperated, you may not want your tone of voice to convey this to your pupil. There are, however, certain times when for safety reasons, you have to get your point across reasonably forcefully. The elements of speech which will help you to communicate effectively are:

- tone of voice;
- use of emphasis;
- content of speech;
- use of figurative language;
- use of humour;
- speed of speaking;
- use of pronunciation;
- pitch of your voice; and
- use of implied speech.

The tone of your voice

When you speak to your pupils it is important to put them at ease and maintain their interest and attention. If they are not paying attention, it is doubtful whether they will learn anything at all.

Your tone of voice conveys your emotions and feelings, such as annoyance and pleasure, and supports the content of what you are saying. As the tone of voice often conveys the true meaning of your message, it is important that you sound friendly and relaxed even though you may be feeling the opposite!

Consider the following question: 'Why did you slow down?'. If you pose this question in a harsh tone of voice, you will sound as though you are telling the pupil off. If you ask the same question with a soft tone of voice, you are showing interest in the pupil's actions.

Practise asking the question in different ways and attempt to convey different meanings to it.

When teaching you need to consider the tone of your voice, not only to give a clearer meaning to the words themselves, but also to add variety to the speech in order to keep the pupil interested and attentive. If you stick to one tone only your voice will become MONOTONOUS, which will soon cause the pupil to lose interest.

The use of emphasis

By putting greater stress on certain words you can alter the meaning of a sentence. For example:

'*What* are you looking for?'
'What *are* you looking for?'
'What are *you* looking for?'
'What are you *looking* for?'
'What are you looking *for*?'

Practise asking this question out loud and, each time, put the emphasis on the word in italics. In the first question, you are asking about the action of looking itself. In the second you imply disbelief that the pupil is bothering to look at all. The third sentence queries whether it is the pupil who should be looking – perhaps somebody else should be looking! In the fourth example you are questioning the action – perhaps there is no point in looking at this moment in time. In the last question you are probing the pupil's understanding of what needs to be seen as a result of looking.

Now try using each of the questions again, continuing to emphasise the word in italics, but try to vary your voice to express concern, anger, and amazement.

As well as saying the words in a particular way you can sometimes stress a particular consonant or vowel to accentuate your meaning. For example, 'Slooowwwlly let the clutch come up'.

People who are practised and skilled speakers, such as politicians or lawyers, often use emphasis to considerable effect not only to help the listener to understand the message but also to indicate hidden meanings, which otherwise might not have been obvious. Sometimes it is only when a speech is heard rather than read that you understand what message is being conveyed.

The content of speech

As well as the tone and emphasis you use when speaking, the words themselves are vital if you wish to be effective in communicating.

The use of an unambiguous vocabulary is vital when teaching people how to drive. You should always try to match the words you are using to the level of understanding and ability of the pupil. The skilled trainer will be able to put trainees at their ease by talking with them at their own level.

> *There is no point in using long and complicated words when teaching somebody who cannot understand them. The best advice is to keep it simple as this is more likely to bring about learning.*

Getting to know your pupils will help you to use suitable words and phrases that they will be able to readily understand. One common criticism of less able instructors is that they tend to use inappropriate phraseology that is not easily understood. The use of jargon should be avoided where possible. If it *is* necessary, make sure that the expressions have been explained to the pupil.

When dealing with the controls of the car it is best to explain to the pupil not only what the control does and how it is used, but the words that you are going to use when dealing with it. This will avoid your pupil becoming confused with possibly dangerous results. For example, if you are going to call the accelerator the gas pedal don't suddenly confuse the pupil by calling it the 'throttle'.

While communicating with pupils, you should avoid talking about race, religion, sex and politics. Remarks of this nature may be offensive to the person in question and, even if they are not, they will devalue whatever else you may be saying, causing the pupil to 'switch off'.

The use of figurative language

Always try to make the content of your message interesting to listen to. There is nothing worse than boring your pupil. You can avoid doing this in a number of ways by using FIGURATIVE LANGUAGE. By this, we mean using such things as:

- METAPHORS;
- SIMILES;
- HYPERBOLE;
- ANALOGIES; and
- PERSONAL EXPERIENCES.

A METAPHOR is used to imply a similarity between things or situations which are not really associated – for example, 'crawling along at a snail's pace'.

A SIMILE is a figurative comparison using terms such as 'like' or 'as'. An example would be to say that a bad driver was 'driving like a lunatic'.

HYPERBOLE is the use of deliberate over-exaggeration – for example, 'That gap is big enough to get a bus through'. (You must be careful when doing this that your pupil does not take you literally!)

An ANALOGY is a comparison made to show a similarity in situations or ideas – for example, 'If you have time to walk across, then you will have time to drive across!'

PERSONAL EXPERIENCES (or ANECDOTES) allow you to compare situations happening now with those that might have happened before. For example, if you had a pupil who tried to emerge unsafely, you might say, 'I had a pupil last week who tried to emerge from a junction without looking. If I hadn't used the dual controls, we would have hit a cyclist!'

By using all of these figures of speech you will make your lessons more interesting and the messages less likely to be forgotten. Care must be taken however that you do not overuse them to the extent that the intended content of your message is diluted or lost.

The use of humour in speech

Instructors who are humorous often maintain their pupils' attention and interest very effectively but it does not work for every pupil or every instructor. If you try to be funny unsuccessfully you could lose your credibility. We all know someone who, when telling a joke, invariably forgets the punchline. You should not tell jokes during the lesson time as this will annoy most pupils, and in no circumstances should you tell racist, sexist, religious or dubious jokes.

Many instructors can be extremely amusing without telling jokes. They can put a message across using wit but, again, not every pupil will respond well to witty remarks and some may take offence, especially if they do not realise that you are trying to be witty. You can often bring a smile to your pupil's face without trying too hard just by being alert and responding to a possibly difficult situation with a humorous remark. For example, you might be waiting at traffic lights which turn to green and your pupil does not move – you could gently ask, 'What colour are we waiting for?'

You should avoid using sarcasm however, as it could cost you a pupil and adds nothing to the learning process.

The speed of speaking

The speed at which you speak can help to maintain the interest of your pupils. You can create anticipation by increasing the speed of speech as you build up to an important point. You can also use silence, or pauses to allow things to sink in before you continue. If you pause while you are talking you can indicate a sense of deliberateness to give emphasis to certain key points. For example: 'MIRROR (pause), SIGNAL (pause), MANOEUVRE'.

You can also use pauses to give you time to think before delivering your next piece of information, but such pauses should not be excessive otherwise you will lose your pupil's attention completely. Try not to fill in the pauses with 'ums' and 'ahs' as this will irritate your pupil and detract from what you are saying.

Slowing down the speed at which you say a single word can be useful in indicating the speed of action required by matching it with the speed of the delivery of the word. For example, 'Slooowwwllyy let the clutch up, squeeeezze the gas' or 'Geennntttly brake'.

The use of pronunciation

It is important that as an 'expert' you pronounce the words you use correctly. Your pupil will expect you to be fully conversant with the subject you are talking about and if you mispronounce too often you could damage your credibility, distract your listeners from what you are saying and reduce their attention. If you come across new words when reading books on driving and intend using them but are unsure of their pronunciation, then it is best to refer to a dictionary.

For example, when teaching the emergency stop many instructors mispronounce the word 'cadence' as in cadence braking. Try looking it up in your dictionary and see if you are pronouncing it correctly!

The pitch of your voice

Pitch is a combination of the tone that you use and the loudness of the sound that you make. Considerable emphasis can be given to the instruction or direction you are giving by varying the pitch of your voice. Pitch is particularly useful when you wish to convey urgency, caution or importance either to whatever it is that you are saying or the way you wish your pupil to react to the words you are using.

Care must be taken not to over-exaggerate the pitch of your voice because it can be a distraction to your pupil. Your speech should be a comfortable variation of harsh and soft tones and of loudness and softness.

Speaking loudly will not always get the attention you desire. You only have to think of British tourists abroad trying to communicate with somebody with no English. In vain they end up almost shouting – '*DO YOU SPEAK ENGLISH?*'!

Pitch is useful when using keyword prompts, particularly those which require urgent action such as 'WAIT', 'HOLD BACK', or 'STOP'.

The use of implied speech

Speech can be used to convey your feelings and especially your attitude to a given situation. The dictionary meaning of the words you are using is not as important as what they imply.

> *It is therefore not only the words being used but also the way in which they are delivered that gets the message across.*

Initial speech will sometimes be used to 'break the ice'. For example, if you ask 'How are you today, Jason?', it not only puts Jason at ease but also gives you some feedback, which might be useful when structuring the lesson content and the way in which you will 'handle' Jason. If he is feeling good, then perhaps you will set the objective for the lesson high. If Jason is not feeling good then perhaps your sights will be lowered to maybe consolidating an existing skill.

When meeting people for the first time, one often talks about the weather or the journey they have had to get to the meeting. The person opening the conversation might not genuinely be interested in these things but is really saying, 'I wish to communicate with you, please respond.'

All of the above elements of speech can be developed. Whether teaching in the car, in the classroom or speaking to larger groups at meetings, conferences, etc, it may be useful either to tape record or, better still (because you can also see what visual impact you are having), video the proceedings with a view to assessing and improving your performance.

There are certain speech distractions which should be eliminated where possible. The most common is the frequent use of speech mannerisms such as, 'OK', 'right', 'you know', 'I mean', 'well then'. This trait gives the impression of a lack of confidence or nervousness, neither of which will help to put the pupil at ease or inspire trust. Also, the use of the word 'right' to mean 'correct' could be misleading and dangerous.

Talking plays a great part in teaching people how to drive and you should take every opportunity to further develop your speaking skills. Remember that, when speaking, you are not only giving a verbal message but also conveying your feelings and attitudes.

> *By varying your speech you can drastically change your listener's interpretation of what you are saying, whether you are talking on a one-to-one basis, or to small or large groups.*

Other common mistakes that speakers make which, particularly when they are talking to groups, can cause their listeners to become bored and lose their concentration are:

● repeating things they have said before; and

● getting too technical for the audience.

Telephone conversations form a valuable part of your life given that the initial contact with a potential customer is often made on the telephone. Much of what has been said about speech also applies.

The problem is that you are unable to read the body language of the person you are speaking to. If you cannot see the gestures and facial expressions of the other party you lose some insight into what they are thinking while they are speaking.

Communicating is not just talking, but should be a two-way exchange of ideas and information. You will therefore need to develop your listening skills.

Developing the communication skills of speaking and listening will help you in presenting a driving lesson. Similar rules will apply to presentations to larger groups but in the next section we are going to concentrate on the one-to-one lesson.

LISTENING SKILLS

We have two ears but only one mouth and we should use them in those proportions. We will learn more about our learners' needs by asking questions and listening to what they say than we will by talking.

You need to pay particular attention to anything that your pupils say voluntarily and try to look at them when they are talking so that you can pick up the silent signals as well. These non-verbal messages will often reinforce the verbal message and help you to understand what people are really feeling. This may often be at variance with what they are saying.

You can then use questions like: 'You don't seem too happy with that. Is there anything that you don't understand?'

When people are listening, they tend to show their interest and attention both verbally and non-verbally. They will nod their heads, lean forward, and say things like, 'Yes, I see', 'That's true', 'I absolutely agree' and 'Hear, hear'.

On the other hand, if they are not listening, they do not look at you, they yawn or they do not respond. Any of these responses will indicate to you that they are bored with the proceedings and that you need to alter your approach to this part of the lesson.

You can develop your listening skills in the following ways:

- 'Listen' with your eyes as well as your ears. By looking at the speaker you will not only hear the words but detect the silent signals which help you to understand the *true* meaning of what the person is saying.

- Ask questions. If anything is unclear, do not be afraid of asking for it to be clarified, and if you disagree with the point being made, then say so, but give your reasons why.

Use open-ended questions to test pupils' understanding of anything you have explained to them and seek their views and opinions on what you are saying. When they respond, hear them out; do not interrupt – wait until they have finished speaking before replying.

Use every lesson that you give as an opportunity to practise your skills as a communicator. At the end of each lesson, you should analyse your own performance with a view to improving your ability. Ask yourself:

- Have I spent enough time looking at and listening to my pupil?
- Have I misinterpreted or not seen any silent signals?
- Have I missed faults of control or observational errors made by my pupil due to not looking at him or her enough?
- Has my own body language been positive or have I put the pupil off by the way in which I have reacted to his or her actions and responses to my questions?
- Could I have communicated with my pupil more effectively today?

BRIEFINGS AND EXPLANATIONS

Driving instructors will often need to give BRIEFINGS to their pupils which explain what is to be covered during the lesson to come. These briefings will usually include a statement of the objectives for the lesson, and a short summary of the key points of WHAT is to be covered.

The briefing will usually be followed by a more full explanation of HOW to do whatever is being taught; WHEN to do it; and, particularly, WHY it is important for the content to be taught in a certain way.

Communicating information of this nature plays a vital part in the normal skill training technique of EXPLANATION, DEMONSTRATION and PRACTICE, which are covered in Chapter 4.

Care must be taken not to 'overload' the pupil. Information should be divided into the following categories:

- MUST KNOW;
- SHOULD KNOW;
- COULD KNOW.

You should be able to identify the 'key points' of the message and then concentrate on making sure that the pupil understands these MUST KNOW elements. Further information from the SHOULD KNOW and COULD KNOW categories may be given in response to questions from the pupil or filled in later, possibly on the move as situations develop which require this further information to be given.

Making sure that pupils know and understand everything that they need to know can be achieved by:

- breaking the information down into its component parts;
- using mnemonics to make routines more memorable – for example, MSM, PSL and LAD:
- using word associations like 'Creep and Peep';
- using visual keys like 'Think of the thickness of a coin';
- slowing or quickening the speed of your speech to match that at which you want the action to be carried out;
- using pauses after important points have been made;
- using the Q/A technique after each key point has been made to confirm the pupil's understanding of what has been said; and
- using visual aids where appropriate and, if the subject is technical, giving hand-outs for pupils to refer to after their lesson.

At the end of each lesson that has contained a briefing or full explanation, assess your own performance. Ask yourself, 'Has the pupil understood all the key points that I have explained?'

Problems will arise during driving lessons if the instructions and directions are not given in a clear and unmistakable manner. You need to take account of all the previous points made about verbal communication but you should also take special note of the following:

- Use language that will be understood by the pupil to avoid any confusion arising.

- Avoid ambiguous words which might be misinterpreted by the pupil. For example: 'Right', meaning OK to correct, could cause the pupil to think you want them to turn right; 'top', meaning top gear, could be misheard as 'stop', especially on a hot day with all the windows down and noise from traffic.

- When on the move give the instruction and directions early enough for the pupil to do whatever is necessary without rushing.

- Match the level of the instruction to the ability of the pupil. A novice will need almost total instruction in what to do, whereas a trained pupil may only need the occasional 'keyword' prompt.

- Use the ALERT–DIRECT–IDENTIFY routine. For example: 'I would like you to...' (ALERT) '... take the next road on the left please.' (DIRECT) 'It's just around the bend.' (IDENTIFY).

Never forget that less-experienced pupils will take longer to react to the instruction or direction. An instruction given too late is likely to result in the pupil:

- missing out important observations;

- losing control with feet or hands;

- assessing situations incorrectly;

- making poor decisions; and

- losing confidence.

When teaching a pupil who is at an advanced stage, you should transfer the responsibility of working out where the various junctions and hazards are by not giving too much help. For many pupils the driving test will be the first opportunity that they have to drive on their own without your help.

A very good way of transferring responsibility and finding out whether the pupil is ready to drive unaccompanied would be to say ten minutes before the end of the lesson: 'Do you think you could find your way back home from here on your own?' If the answer is yes, then let the pupil drive back without any instructions or directions being given.

Once the pupil is nearly at driving test standard you should make sure that you use phraseology similar to that of the examiner as a way of preparing for the test situation. It is extremely important that you 'sit in' on a driving test occasionally so that you can reaffirm your understanding of how an examiner gives directional instructions and the timing of them.

One of the most common criticisms of ADI's is that of over-instruction. This happens because the instructor does not know when to 'drop out'. Are you guilty of 'over-instructing'? If so, what are you going to do about it?

At the end of each lesson you will need to ask yourself:

- Were the instructions and directions given to my pupil in a clear and unmistakable manner?

- Did the timing of the directions given allow the pupil to do all the things necessary to deal with situations?

- Was there any ambiguity in the instructions and directions given?

BODY LANGUAGE

Whenever we communicate with others, we use body language – it is unavoidable and instinctive. Speech and the development of language began about 500,000 years ago but it is probable that body language has been used for at least one million years.

Because body language is so deeply ingrained in us, it is difficult to disguise and even when you are not speaking you are sending messages to others, sometimes without even being aware of it. Your physical appearance, posture, gestures, gaze and facial expressions indicate to others your moods and feelings.

> *It is important for driving instructors to be able to use positive body language and interpret the body language of their learners.*

Because the body language of your learners may give you more information about their mood and receptiveness than what they are saying, being able to interpret accurately these silent signals will assist you in deciding whether to modify your delivery, back off, or even change the activity entirely. For example, should the face of your pupil show frustration when failing to master a reversing exercise, you may decide to switch to something that is less demanding in order to boost the pupils' confidence rather than destroy it.

The ability to interpret body language will also enable you to tell whether there is any difference between what the pupil is saying and what they really think. The driving instructor needs to develop a high degree of perceptual sensitivity to read accurately the silent signals being sent by pupils.

Body language is particularly important in interviewing, negotiating, selling and buying situations. Although the general rules regarding body language will apply at meetings, in the classroom or during social encounters, when you are giving driving lessons your skills will need to be adapted to take account of the fact that, on the move, you can only see the side of your pupil's face. (We do not encourage our pupils to look at us while they are driving!) Of course, while stationary you will often be able to see their eyes as well.

If you want to be able to use your own body language in a positive way and be able to read that of others, you need to recognise the constituents of it. There are seven main constituents, some of which are more relevant to driving instruction than others:

- FACIAL EXPRESSIONS;
- GAZE;
- POSTURE;
- GESTURES;
- PROXIMITY;
- TOUCH; and
- PERSONAL APPEARANCE.

When teaching in the car, you will need to spend much time not only reading the road ahead but looking at the face, eyes, hands and feet of pupils. Although the hands and feet will tell how well the controls are being used, the face and eyes will not only show where pupils are looking but also what they may be thinking or feeling.

Facial expressions

In driving instruction facial expressions are most useful. The face is highly visible (even in profile) and is capable of conveying one's innermost feelings. Think of the expression on the face of someone who has just failed the driving test and then compare it with that of someone else who has just passed!

The face is a very spontaneous communicator of messages and will generally convey the feelings of its owner in a uniform way. The face is, therefore, a fairly reliable indicator of happiness or despair, pain or pleasure. Consequently, when teaching, you should ensure that your facial expressions do not contradict what you are saying – if they do, it will have a disturbing effect on your pupils.

Gaze

When explaining things to your pupil, or debriefing at the side of the road, or in a classroom situation, you will normally have eye-to-eye contact. The eyes can tell you a great deal about what people may be feeling but, with skill and practice, your eyes can tell others what you want them to think you are feeling. Poker players and salesmen use this technique to good effect, sometimes with high stakes to play for.

A strong gaze usually shows that you are being attentive and concentrating on what the other person is saying. However, in some cultures it isseen to be impolite to stare. When people become embarrassed they will often break eye contact and look away.

Breaking eye contact may show that you have made an error or cannot answer a question, while a reluctance to look at someone at all may show your dislike or distrust of that person.

However, establishing strong eye contact will show that you have a genuine desire to communicate and will be seen by your pupils as an invitation to speak. It is a cultural expectation that people look at each other when communicating. If you are reluctant to look someone in the face when talking to them, or continually shift your eyes around, you will not inspire trust.

Your emotions, attitudes and honesty, as portrayed by your eye contact, make gaze an important constituent of your body language. Aggressive stares and shifty looks should be avoided. You should try to develop a strong gaze, with an occasional blink or look away which will make people feel more comfortable and receptive.

Posture

In the confined space of a motor car, when your feet and hands are occupied, posture is not quite so revealing as in a classroom situation where how you stand or sit and the position of your arms and legs will reflect your feelings and attitudes to others.

A normal seating position, which allows the pupil to reach the foot and hand controls comfortably, will of course determine the 'angles' of their legs and arms.

You can display a warmth and liking for someone by leaning towards them slightly, with your arms relaxed. You can show your disgust at their actions by turning away and looking out of the window. You must be careful not to hover over the dual controls with your feet as this will unnerve pupils and destroy their self-confidence. You should avoid continually looking round to check the blindspots on the move for the same reason. Careful and subtle use of your dual mirrors will achieve the same objective but without worrying the pupil.

In meetings or in the classroom, your posture becomes much more important. An erect posture will indicate a sense of pride, confidence and self-discipline, while stooping shoulders and head down may be interpreted as being slovenly or lacking in confidence. Your impressions of others and their impressions of you will be influenced by posture and gait. When walking across the room, you should therefore adopt a confident purposeful walk, which will indicate self-assurance, confidence and personal dynamism.

When giving presentations, you can use posture and body movements to help to bring your story to life, supporting any verbal message, thus maintaining the interest of those who are watching and listening.

Gestures

Gestures may occasionally be used instead of words in certain circumstances. If you are trying to communicate with a deaf person or someone who does not speak English, gestures will help you to communicate. Your hands can be used to demonstrate how the clutch plates come together, for example.

A nod of the head, or a wave of the hand are friendly, passive signals which may be given to other instructors or road-users to acknowledge a courtesy, whereas a shaking of the fist conveys aggression. Sometimes your gestures will be involuntary. For example, scratching your head or chin may signal that you are uneasy or concerned about what your pupil is doing. Driving instructors who constantly fidget or wave their arms about will give their pupils the impression that they are nervous or worried. This will do little to build up pupils' confidence! Gesticulations of this nature or pen waving while going along the road will also distract the pupil from concentrating on the road and could be dangerous.

To control them, you need to be aware of your gestures, especially those that may be distracting to others. If you give presentations at meetings or in the classroom, a videotape of your performance will be invaluable in helping you to recognise those gestures that are weak and those that are effective in emphasising and reinforcing your verbal messages. If you are uncomfortable using deliberately planned gestures, rehearsal and practice will allow you to deliver them in such a way that they appear to be spontaneous and natural rather than forced and awkward.

Proximity (personal space)

The driving instructor should be aware that each pupil needs a certain amount of personal space (a 'space bubble') with which they feel comfortable. Encroaching on this personal space may make the pupil feel uncomfortable, and could even cause them to change to a different driving instructor.

You need to make sure that this space is not so great that your teaching loses its effectiveness. The following diagram shows the different environments and situations and the amount of space required.

You will see from the diagram that the driving instructor is in the privileged position of being allowed to get closer than almost everybody else, with the exception perhaps of the family doctor!

ENVIRONMENT		SPACE REQUIRED
In the car		A few inches
With close friends and relatives, spouses and children		About 18 inches or 45 cms
Social functions	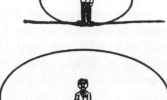	About 45 to 120 cms
In the classroom, with strangers or at business meetings		Public space of between 120 cms and 3 metres
When giving a lecture or talking at a conference		Lecturer space of at least 3 metres

The space bubble

The amount of personal space required is sometimes dependent on the cultural background of the person. In many Mediterranean countries and in Norway, for example, people feel comfortable almost rubbing shoulders. For most British people this would be quite unacceptable.

You will need to be very sensitive to the needs of each individual pupil in this respect and generally should avoid getting too close wherever possible. This can be difficult in a small car, especially if both you and the pupil are quite large!

In the classroom, distance can be a barrier to communication, as can speaking from behind a desk, or up on a rostrum. Avoid being seen as authoritarian and try to establish an informal atmosphere. For instance, it can sometimes be more effective to sit on the edge of the desk than behind it.

Touch

Formal touches are important when meeting someone for the first time, like a new pupil. A firm (but not crushing) handshake will indicate self-confidence which is especially important when a male meets another male. A limp, handshake implies weakness and it would be better not to give one at all.

At the end of a lesson a handshake is not really necessary and a wave or pat on the back might be more effective. These can also be nice gestures when the pupil passes the driving test.

You must be extremely careful not to touch pupils in the car unless it is for reasons of safety. Touching pupils may make them feel uncomfortable or threatened and cause them to distrust your motives. Pupils often change instructors because unnecessary physical contact upsets them.

Cultural backgrounds sometimes influence the desire to touch and be touched. For example, people from the Greek island of Rhodes continually touch each other during conversation so, if you have a pupil from this lovely island, watch out!

If a pupil has just received some distressing news you might feel tempted to give them a hug but, generally, a sympathetic ear is just as effective and certainly less likely to be misinterpreted as a social advance.

Personal appearance

When you are a driving instructor, from the moment you leave home to the moment you return back at the end of the day, you are under scrutiny from the public, particularly if you have your name on the car! Your appearance, dress and grooming may create an initial impression that is very difficult to change.

When considering body language, your personal appearance, hair and the clothes that you wear are of great importance because you may well have more control over them than your facial features and posture. There is little we can do to change our shape, features and size, but much can be done to improve our appearance, the suitability of our clothes and the general impression that we convey.

When teaching people to drive, you do of course have to take account of the weather conditions and, while it might not be necessary to wear a three-piece suit, you can still dress casually but smartly. In the summer and winter you will need to dress for comfort, but never forget that your appearance can influence your impact on people and can help to create a favourable or an unfavourable impression.

Propriety of dress is particularly important for the female instructor to help overcome possible problems with male pupils who might see revealing clothes, together with the natural caring attitude of the teacher, as an invitation to develop social relationships.

Pupils' body language

All the constituents of body language that we have discussed in the previous section may combine to present a positive image to those you come into contact with.

It is equally important that you recognise the silent signals your pupils give out. We have chosen common signs that your pupils may give you to indicate the way they feel. Getting to know your pupils better will assist you in accurately interpreting their body language. Generally speaking, the following rules apply.

Pupils who are willing to listen:

- sit with their head on one side;
- look directly at you;
- rest their chin on the palm of their hand;
- nod in agreement;
- say things like 'I see'.

Pupils who are pleased:

- smile;
- use strong eye contact;
- can't stop talking;
- use humour in their speech;
- are polite and courteous.

Pupils who are anxious to ask a question:

- lift a hand or finger;
- shift their sitting position;
- fidget with their ear or chin;
- look intently at you with their head on one side.

Pupils who are annoyed with themselves:

- shake their heads;
- tightly cross their arms;
- hit the steering wheel;
- exhale loudly;
- frown.

Pupils who have had a fright:

- cover their eyes with their hands;
- open their mouth and put their head back;
- bite their bottom lip;
- become red in the face;
- inhale sharply.

Pupils who are disappointed:

- frown or scowl;
- drop their shoulders and let their head drop forwards;
- let their arms fall into their lap;
- droop their mouth.

Pupils who are nervous:

- talk incessantly about nothing;
- tighten their grip on the steering wheel;
- lick their lips;
- bite their nails or chew their fingers.

Looking at your pupils will not only allow you to see and interpret their body language, but also assist you in identifying faults being made which involve their feet, hands and eyes. If you do not see the fault, how can you suggest a remedy for it?

FEEDBACK

Feedback is an important part of the learning process. A simple example is where, for example, the driver hears an ambulance approaching from behind and pulls over to let it pass. Another example would be when the 'feel' from a flat tyre alerts the driver to the fact that something is wrong.

Giving and gaining feedback are useful PTS, especially when teaching on a one-to-one basis or in small groups.

Feedback is usually preceded by an enquiry, a prompt or a physical action. For example, the facial expression of pupils after having carried out a manoeuvre will often give a good indication of how well they feel they have done.

Feedback is obtained and 'fed back' to the initial prompter as a direct result of the initial action. It can be given verbally, physically or sometimes by body language, and can relate both to people and machinery.

In the driving instruction experience, feedback can occur from:

- the car to the pupil/instructor, eg engine labouring;
- the pupil to the instructor;
- the instructor to the pupil;
- the pupil to other road users;
- other road users to the pupil;
- the examiner to the pupil;

- the pupil to the examiner;
- the trainer to the trainee;
- the trainee to the trainer.

Using a question-and-answer routine is only one way of giving and obtaining feedback.

When teaching learner drivers you should give feedback on what they are doing well and what may need improving. Just as important is finding out from pupils how well *they* think they are doing. They might think they are doing brilliantly when they are really struggling. Alternatively, pupils might think they need extra tuition on a particular topic, whereas you might think this is unnecessary. Every pupil will benefit from extra lessons, so never discourage them from booking more if they feel they need them.

Many driving instructors do not understand feedback and give instead constant criticism, which only destroys what confidence pupils may have and leaves them feeling dejected and wanting to give up.

Many potentially good drivers give up because they do not receive support and encouragement from their instructors. Invariably these pupils will start learning again, as they really need to drive. However, they nearly always go to a different instructor. Never forget that if you are not fulfilling the needs of your pupils, there are plenty more instructors for them to choose from.

Feedback should therefore be offered in a sensitive way, so as not to hurt the feelings of the pupil.

A number of guidelines need to be followed when giving feedback to your pupils.

- Feedback should always focus on what actually happened rather than on what should or might have happened.
- Suggest that pupils comment on their own performance before giving feedback. They will often be more self-critical than you expected.
- Make sure that you balance pupils' strengths and weaknesses.
- Concentrate on areas where you know that the pupil are capable of improvement; don't dwell on points that you know they are not able to alter. This is most important when pupils are aware that they have limitations.
- Be helpful rather than sounding judgmental. For example, rather than saying 'You will fail your test if you do that', you could try 'Your passengers will have a much more comfortable ride if you do this'.
- Try to 'round off' any feedback by stressing the good points.
- Above all, feedback should be seen by pupils as being constructive and positive.

Hopefully the guidelines above will help you to give feedback in a 'human' way, as this will build the confidence of your pupils and their confidence in your ability to teach!

After each lesson, analyse any feedback you have given. Decide whether you could have improved the way in which you presented the feedback to your pupil.

Think carefully about how your pupil reacted to the feedback. Did you tell the pupil what he or she had done well or did you just criticise their driving?

4

Lesson planning

PRESENTING THE LESSON

Any presentation is much more likely to achieve its objectives if the presenter has done sufficient preparation.

The danger in having no plan is, as Rudyard Kipling once said, 'If you don't know where you are going, no road will lead you there!'

In Chapter 7 we cover the specific requirements for presenting a lesson during the ADI Part 3 test. In that situation, the supervising examiner will actually set the objectives for the lesson and determine the character of the pupil. There is also a limitation on the time available for the lesson.

With a real pupil on a real driving lesson, it is your responsibility to set the objectives and plan the use of time, taking into account the specific needs of the pupil. You usually have the advantage of knowing your pupil.

The best way to plan a lesson is first of all to think of the pupil and their level of ability. Then ask yourself the crucial 'teaching' questions – WHAT?, WHY?, HOW?, WHERE? and WHEN?

- What does the pupil already know?

- What are we going to teach, and Why do we need to teach it?

- How are we going to get the message across?

- Where do we need to go to carry out the main part of the lesson, and When should we get to the main content of the lesson?

- How are we going to manage the time available?

Only when you have answered all of these questions can you get to work in planning the lesson and delivering the presentation.

In any teaching/learning situation the lesson should be structured. This is known as PUPIL-CENTRED LEARNING. For you and your pupil to achieve your separate objectives, you will need to involve the pupil, and the following communication skills will help you to do this.

> *You should start each lesson with a clear idea of WHAT you are going to teach and WHY you are going to teach it, WHERE the lesson is going to take place, HOW the timetable is to be utilised and HOW the lesson is going to be structured.*

At the start of a Check Test, the examiner will often ask the instructor, 'What is your lesson plan for today?' It is not unusual for the reply to be, 'Well, I just thought we would drive around for a bit and see how things develop'!

Professional driving instruction should not be a matter of driving around for a bit to see what develops. The good instructor should:

● have a clearly defined plan of what is going to be taught;

● take into account the level of ability of the pupil when setting the objectives for the lesson to be given; and

● know in advance what activities are going to take place during the lesson and how the pupil is going to be kept interested and attentive.

A grade six instructor will probably go a lot further than that and would be likely to:

● have specified learning goals for the student;

● vary the teaching methods to suit those goals and the characteristics of the student;

● demonstrate a range of skills when using these teaching methods and any visual or learning aids;

● carefully manage the time, structure and content of the lesson;

● adapt the lesson to suit the perceived needs of the student where necessary;

● identify, analyse and correct faults;

● identify any problem areas, taking remedial action or recommending further training where necessary;

- comply with DSA examination requirements when appropriate;

- take account of the safety of the student, the passenger and any other road-users at all times;

- offer feedback to the student during and at the end of the lesson, where appropriate;

- link forward to the next lesson; and

- evaluate what learning has taken place.

Your lesson plan may need to be changed if problems are encountered as the lesson progresses. For example, you might plan to teach the pupil how to carry out one of the manoeuvres but, on the way to a suitable place, the pupil fails to see a pedestrian who is just about to step onto a pedestrian crossing. This causes you to have to use the dual controls.

In view of the seriousness of the error, it would make sense to postpone the original manoeuvre planned and spend some time on dealing with how to approach pedestrian crossings, stopping when necessary.

This should not present any problems for the learner as long as you explain why the lesson plan has been changed, and that the original subject will be covered in a future lesson.

The following is an example of a formal lesson plan.

Lesson plan

Partly trained pupil

Instruction in turning the car round to face the opposite way using forward and reverse gears.

Objectives

By the end of the lesson the pupil will be able to:

1) choose an appropriate site for the manoeuvre;
2) coordinate the controls with reasonable smoothness;
3) take effective observation before and during the manoeuvre;
4) carry out the manoeuvre with reasonable accuracy.

Note that in the lesson plan on page 72, the timings are only a guide and will vary depending on the pupil's knowledge, response and receptiveness.

Taking account of the individual needs of the pupil, the lesson plan will also need to be linked in with:

● matching the level of instruction to the ability of the pupil; and

● route selection and planning.

TIME	MAIN POINTS AND METHOD	TEACHING AIDS
4–8 minutes approx	Q/A recap and briefing: explanation of manoeuvre	'DRIVING' diagram
5–10 minutes approx	Demonstration if appropriate, then full talk-through practice	
5 minutes approx	Debriefing, feedback, encouragement, praise, fault analysis	'DRIVING' diagram if appropriate
5–10 minutes approx	Remedial practice; prompts if necessary	
5 minutes	Debriefing, feedback, encouragement, praise, fault analysis, link forward to next lesson	

To appreciate the extent of the task that faces you, consider how you would plan a lesson for each of the potential pupils listed below – what type of routes you would choose and how you would vary your level of instruction.

● An absolute beginner.

● A partly trained pupil.

● A pupil at about 'L' test standard.

● Somebody who has recently passed the 'L' test but has never driven on motorways.

● Somebody who passed the 'L' test a few years ago but has not driven since.

● A full licence holder who wishes to take the IAM or RoSPA advanced test.

● A company driver taking a 'defensive driving' course.

- The holder of a full foreign licence who has never driven in this country or on the left-hand side of the road.

- Somebody who is just about to appear in court on a traffic offence and who needs an asessement and report.

- Somebody who has to take a test as part of a court order.

- Somebody who has to take an *extended* test as part of a court order.

At the end of each driving lesson, you should ask yourself:

- Did the lesson plan help the student to achieve the objectives stated at the beginning of the lesson?

- Did I involve the pupil in the lesson sufficiently?

- Should I have changed the lesson plan to take account of perceived problems?

- Did I give the pupil enough feedback on how well they were doing?

- Did I plan the lesson thoroughly?

- Were the routes chosen correctly?

- Was the level of instruction pitched appropriately for the pupil?

- With hindsight, was there anything I should have done differently?

TEACHING BY OBJECTIVES

The theory of teaching by objectives is covered in more detail in *The Driving Instructor's Handbook*. In this section of the book, we will be explaining how to put the theory into practice, using your practical teaching skills. General objectives give the teaching goals. These tend to be broken down into more specific objectives, which allow the pupil to demonstrate his or her attainment of those goals.

In Chapter 21 we covered: learning to memorise something; learning to understand something; learning to do something; and attitude development. When teaching someone how to drive, it is not very helpful to separate these activities. The learner needs to practise all of the above, and then reflect on the experience with guidance from the instructor.

Driving instructors are rather like baby-sitters. They spend time with their charges for perhaps only one or two hours a week. As soon as the children they are looking after can fend for themselves, the babysitter is no longer required. Once learner drivers have passed the 'L' test, they have no further need for their driving instructors and will possibly never seen them again unless they are persuaded to take some extra training under the Pass Plus scheme or in preparation for one of the advanced driving tests.

Given the limitations of time and money, all we can hope to achieve when teaching our learners is that they know 'where they are going, and how they are going to get there'.

There will probably be big gaps in their knowledge, understanding, skills and their attitude may need modifying from time to time. They will undoubtedly take risks along the way, but, hopefully, they will learn from the experience.

So, faced with this problem, how can we make the best use of the short amount of time available for teaching? We need to ask ourselves:

● What are our pupils setting out to achieve?

● What is the best way of helping them to achieve it in the time available?

If we are absolutely honest with ourselves, the answers to these questions will probably be 'pass the "L" test' and 'plan a course of lessons linked to the requirements of the test'.

Because of the public perception about 'passing the test' it is often left to the instructors to use their professional skills to persuade their pupils that the main objective of a course of lessons is to teach '*safe driving for life*'.

Whatever the type of course or subject matter, the objectives for each particular pupil will need to be clearly defined and stated.

Teaching by objectives, or using a 'stepping stone' approach, will make the learning process more enjoyable for pupils in that they will be able to recognise and measure how their skills are progressing against the requirements of the 'L' test.

One of the biggest problems for learners when they first start their lessons is that they have a feeling of insecurity. This is due largely to them not being able to compare their progress, or lack of it, with that of their peers, who may also be learning to drive.

Using a stepping-stone approach leading up to the test does help to overcome this problem. When they have achieved one objective, then they move on to the next one, and so on. If they are unable to achieve an objective, then this is where your skill as a teacher is put to the test. You will have to find the right method for your pupil – one which ensures that each one will learn something. Knowing when to encourage, praise, question, explain, demonstrate and assess are the skills of the teacher.

It is essential to remember that there is no such thing as a bad learner. The inability of the pupil to learn is much more likely to be the fault of the teacher! Your skill will be to set the objectives for the pupil at an appropriate level, so as to give the pupil a realistic target. When the target is hit, the pupil should feel a sense of achievement, which will stimulate the desire to make more progress.

The most important factor in the selection of objectives is that both the instructor and the pupil agree what they are to be, and that some record is kept of progress made. Using this system gives an immediate progress chart for each pupil and will also act as a memory prompt for you so that you will be able to remember which particular item is the next one to be covered.

By using a log book or progress report, another instructor would be able to pick up where the previous instructor has left off.

As well as giving each pupil feedback on their progress on a record or appointment card, you should also keep a master list in the car so that each pupil's progress can be monitored. Progress sheets can be filed on a clip board in alphabetical order by surname.

Do not lose sight of the fact that as well as giving pupils an individual 'test-related' programme of learning, we are also preparing them for a lifetime of safe driving. The requirements of the test go further than performing the set exercises. Knowledge, understanding and attitude all come into it as well as practical skill. Your course of instruction should cover all of these.

In using objectives based on the DSA syllabus we are giving our learners a firm foundation. Drivers will reflect on their performance long after they have passed the driving test. There will undoubtedly be gaps which are likely to be filled as they gain experience.

The LEARNING CIRCLE of learning, practice and reflection which we saw in Chapter 21 will hold good for the rest of their driving lives!

When teaching by objectives you will need to ask yourself at the end of each lesson:

● Have I set the objectives at a realistic level for the pupil?

● Am I concentrating too much on 'getting them through the test' instead of teaching safe driving for life?

● Am I paying enough attention to knowledge, understanding and attitude, or spending too much time on skill training?

● Have I kept my pupil's progress chart or log book up to date?

● Have I kept my own progress chart for this pupil up to date?

LEVELS OF INSTRUCTION

In most driving lessons, the professional instructor will be involved in the following activities:

● teaching new skills;

● consolidating partly learnt skills; and

● assessing skills already learnt or partly learnt.

Some lessons may contain a mixture of some or all of these. Many instructors make the mistake of trying to cram too many activities into one lesson to the detriment of the learning process.

As well as planning the content of the lesson to be given, you need to consider carefully the routes and areas chosen and the level of instruction required for each particular pupil.

One of the problems for instructors is knowing when to 'drop out' and transfer to the pupil the responsibility for solving problems and making decisions. The sooner your pupils start to think things out and make decisions for themselves, the sooner they will be ready to drive unaccompanied.

For many learners, the first time they ever drive 'unaccompanied' will be on the 'L' test, when the examiner is there purely as an observer.

The skilful instructor knows when to stop talking. Of course, in most driving lessons, you will need to give directions but, during the lessons immediately before the test, it would be very beneficial to the learner if you say, 'Let's see if you can drive home on your own, without me saying anything at all. You make all the decisions and pretend that I am not here.' You would, of course, need to be sure that your pupil knew the way home.

In this situation, the only time you should intervene is for safety reasons. This exercise will boost the confidence of the pupil coming up to the test, and also give you a measure of the pupil's readiness to drive unaccompanied. At the end of the 'unaccompanied drive' it will be useful to ask the pupil: 'How did you feel about driving on your own then?'

Some feedback would then need to be given to the pupil. A requirement for more lessons might be necessary. Two very common instructional errors arise from instructors not matching the level of instruction to suit the level of ability of their pupil. This can take the form of over- or under-instruction.

Over-instruction

This often occurs when the instructor is teaching a new skill, or who has identified a problem area and is giving the pupil a complete 'talk-through' on a subject. The new skill will probably be mixed in with the skills that are already learnt or partly learnt.

For example, the instructor may be talking the pupil through a difficult junction, with the added problem of road-works. When the junction has been negotiated, the pupil is asked to pull in and park somewhere convenient, so that they can discuss what happened. The instructor forgets that the pupil knows how to park unaccompanied and says: 'Gently brake to slow; clutch down; gently brake to stop; apply the handbrake; select neutral'.

The pupil may have parked a hundred times unaided, without any problem. What has happened is that the instructor, who has got so involved in the 'talk-through' mode, has forgotten when to keep quiet.

You should therefore try to restrict your prompted practice or talk-through to those aspects of driving which are new to the pupil, or which are as yet unaccomplished. Over-instruction is particularly common when the pupil is approaching test standard. It is as if the instructor is reluctant to 'let go of the reins'. Always remember that at this level your pupils will learn a lot more by doing it themselves, even if they get it wrong, than by listening to you telling them what to do.

Under-instruction

This is particularly common when the pupil is in the novice stage or is only partially trained. When teaching new skills you need to control the practice so that, where possible, the pupil gets it right first time. There is nothing more motivating for the pupil than success, even though that success may be the result of you prompting or talking them through the task. Your function is to talk the pupil through each stage of the operation, skill or exercise until they develop the ability and confidence to do it for themselves.

The need for a full-talk through is greatest in the early stages of learning a particular task so as to lessen the risk of vehicle abuse and inconvenience or danger to other road-users.

The talk-through must give the pupil enough time to interpret and execute your instructions comfortably. The speed with which each pupil will be able to do this is likely to vary. You therefore need to match the level of instruction and the timing of your delivery to the particular needs of the pupil.

Knowing when to drop out is important. If you leave the pupil on his or her own too soon, resulting in a poor execution of the task, it can be very demotivating. However, when you consider the pupil is ready to take personal responsibility, you should encourage them to do so. Some pupils will need lots of encouragement to act and think for themselves. Others will make rapid progress when left to work on their own initiative.

You might need to change from 'talk-through' mode to 'prompted practice' mode. Prompting is the natural progression from controlled practice and will largely depend on the ability and willingness of pupils to make decisions for themselves.

If conditions become too busy for the pupil's ability or if potential danger is a factor, then the pupil may be reluctant to make any decisions at all. Where these situations arise you must be prepared to step in and prompt when required.

The use of detailed instructions should decrease as the ability of the pupil increases, thereby transferring the responsibility from you to them for making decisions and acting on them.

In the last few lessons leading up to the driving test, it should not be necessary for you to prompt the pupil at all. If this is not the case, then you have a selling job to do. You need to either sell more lessons and the necessity for further practice or postponement of the test.

At the end of each lesson ask yourself:

- Did I match the level of the instruction given to the ability of the pupil?

- Did I over-instruct on things that the pupil should need no instruction on?

- Did I leave the pupil to do things without prompting or should I have given more help?

ROUTE PLANNING

Route selection and planning is itself a *practical teaching skill* and is an essential part of lesson preparation and planning. Part of an instructor's role is to create a situation in which learning can take place, and the selection of routes is an integral element in this process.

The ideal route would be one that takes account of the character and level of ability of the pupil. It should be designed to stretch them but not be daunting.

Using training routes which are not relevant to the needs of the pupil or not appropriate to the requirements of the lesson plan can have an extremely negative effect on the training.

The confidence of some learners is destroyed because they are taken into difficult situations which require good clutch control before they have mastered this skill. Imagine how you would feel if you were sitting at a red traffic light on your first driving lesson and you stalled the engine a couple of times!

If new drivers are unnecessarily exposed to road and traffic conditions with which they are unable to cope, it is quite likely that the amount of learning taking place will be reduced. In the most extreme case, the pupil's confidence will be severely affected, with a detrimental effect on learning or even a reversal of the learning process.

At the other end of the scale, restricting the experienced learner to inappropriate basic routes will not encourage them to develop their skills.

When planning routes, you should consider some of the main requirements:

- the specific objectives for the lesson;
- the standard and ability of the pupil combined with the need to introduce or improve any skill or procedure;
- any particular weaknesses or strengths of the pupil;
- any hazards or features that you may want to include or avoid in the overall lesson plan;
- the length of time available for the lesson;
- whether any danger or inconvenience might be caused by using a particular area at a particular time; and
- if any unnecessary or excessive nuisance would be caused to local residents.

Ideally, you should have a thorough knowledge of the training area and any local traffic conditions. However, as this is not always practicable or possible, you will need to take care to avoid any extreme conditions.

If, because of the local geography and the limited time available, complex situations cannot be avoided, consider whether you should drive the pupil to a more appropriate training area. In this event, use the drive to give a demonstration of any relevant points and to include a 'talk-through' of what you are doing.

Training routes and areas tend to fall into three main categories: nursery or basic, intermediate and advanced. There will not be a clear division between the three groups and there will often be a considerable overlap from one group to another. Nevertheless, it is important that you have a clear idea of the appropriate routes within your own working environment.

Nursery Routes – These will normally include fairly long, straight, wide roads without too many parked vehicles and avoiding pedestrian crossings, traffic lights and roundabouts. This type of route will incorporate progressively most or all of the following features:

- roads that are long enough to allow for a reasonable progression through all the gears and for stopping from various speeds;
- several upward and downward gradients suitable for starting and stopping;

- left- and right-hand bends to develop speed adjustment and gear changing skills;
- left turns from main roads to side roads;
- left turns from side roads to main roads; and
- right turns into side roads and onto main roads.

Intermediate Routes – These should include busier junctions and general traffic conditions. At this stage, try to avoid dual carriageways, multi-lane roads and any one-way systems. Some or all of the following features might be incorporated in the routes:

- crossroads and junctions with 'stop' and 'give way' signs;
- several uphill, give-way junctions;
- traffic lights and basic roundabouts; and
- areas for manoeuvring.

Care should be taken to avoid too many complicated traffic situations – for example, right turns onto exceptionally busy main roads or complex junctions.

Advanced Routes – These will incorporate most of the features of the intermediate routes and should be extended to give a wider variety of traffic and road conditions. They should include, where possible, dual carriageways, multi-lane roads and one-way systems as well as residential, urban and rural roads. A properly planned 'advanced' route will provide the opportunity to conduct mock tests without using actual test routes. You should be able to find routes that include:

- different types of pedestrian crossings;
- roads with varying speed limits;
- level crossings, dual carriageways and one-way streets;
- multi-laned roads for lane selection and lane discipline; and
- rural, urban and residential roads.

Starting with nursery routes, try to introduce new elements and situations at a controlled rate bearing in mind the needs of pupils and the level of their ability. Get used to what seems to be 'their own pace' – one at which they feel comfortable.

There may be occasions when a mixture of all types of route may be incorporated into one lesson – for example, when making an initial assessment of a new pupil who has previous driving experience.

Ideally, you should start off with a fairly wide selection of routes. This will give you the opportunity to vary and extend them with experience. Retain a certain amount of flexibility in using the planned routes because you may, for instance, need to spend more time than anticipated on a topic that the pupil is finding more difficult than expected.

If a specific problem is identified, you may need to demonstrate or contrive to bring the pupil back to a particular junction in order to 'recreate' a situation.

Excessive repetition of identical routes will often lead to a lack of interest or response from the pupil. This in turn will lead to slow progress in learning and may also be counterproductive. Some variation of routes is essential to the learning process and will sustain the pupil's interest and motivation. Occasionally, however, you may decide that a certain amount of repetition is necessary to work on a specific task relevant to the objectives for a particular lesson.

Remember that training routes are often a compromise between the ideal and the reality of local conditions in the training area. The nature of traffic conditions can vary enormously from time to time and from lesson to lesson. You may find that a carefully planned route may unexpectedly prove unsuitable and you are faced with a situation that the pupil is not ready for. Careful route planning can, however, keep these incidents to a manageable level. Be ready to extend the length of a lesson for a particular pupil if appropriate training routes are not readily available in the immediate vicinity.

At the end of each lesson, ask yourself:

- Did I choose a route that was suitable for the level of ability of the pupil and for the objectives stated?
- Did I vary the route sufficiently to sustain the interest of the pupil?
- Am I using routes which stretch the ability of the pupil but without destroying their confidence?

FAULT ASSESSMENT

This section deals with fault recognition, assessment and correction.

Driving faults normally fall into two separate categories: in car (control skills) and outside the car (road procedure errors).

You will often find that 'in-car' errors will lead to errors of road procedure, lack of accuracy or failure to respond correctly to traffic situations

You will need to use your eyes, dividing your attention between what is happening on the road ahead, what is happening behind and what your pupil is doing with their hands, feet and eyes.

Try not to:

● watch the pupil so intently that you miss important changes in the traffic situation ahead to which your pupil should be responding; or

● watch the road and traffic so intently that you miss faults that are happening in the car.

An effective way of coping with all the visual checks required is to use the MSM, PSL, LAD routines, but from an instructional point of view. For example, when approaching a hazard you should check that your pupil:

M – checks the rear view mirrors; look in your own mirror to confirm what is happening behind; check that your pupil acts sensibly on what is seen;
S – is signalling properly, when necessary and at the correct time;
M – carries out the manoeuvre correctly;

becomes:

P – positions the vehicle correctly for the situation;
S – slows down to a suitable speed and selects an appropriate gear when nece sary;
L – is looking early enough, at the correct time, and that looking is effective and includes using the mirrors;

becomes:

A – assesses the situation correctly;
D – makes a good decision as to how to deal with the hazard.

Continuous assessment should be sensitive to the pupil's needs and is concerned with improving performance. In the last few lessons leading up to the 'L' test, the continuous assessment should give way to 'objective' or 'mock' testing. The purpose of this is to assess the pupil's readiness to take the test and it should be matched to the requirements of the test itself.

Grading of errors

Try not to think of errors as being black or white. In driving, there are many shades of grey, and the circumstances surrounding the error need to be taken into account. When assessing driver error, you should take into consideration the following:

● an error can involve varying degrees of importance; and

- some errors are of a more serious nature and can result in more severe consequences than others.

Driver errors will generally fall into one of four categories:

1. **Not marked** – This is where the fault is so slight that you decide not to mention it.
2. **Minor** – This is where the fault does not involve a serious or dangerous situation. No other road-user is involved either potentially or actually.
3. **Serious** – A serious fault is one which involves potential risk to persons or property.
4. **Dangerous** – This is where the actions of the pupil cause actual danger to persons or property.

There is a need for some standardisation between the consistency of assessments made during driving lessons and those used for the driving test. Full details of the Driving Standards Agency fault assessment categories can be found in *The Driving Instructor's Handbook*.

Having said this, there is no necessity for you to grade errors exactly to DSA test criteria. Remember that we are teaching safe driving for life. Consequently, some instructors may aim for a much higher overall standard of ability than that required on the 'L' test.

This can be beneficial to their pupils. It would be true to say that most learners do not perform as well on the driving test as they do while out with their instructor on lessons. Pupils who hve been trained to a higher standard should therefore stand a better chance of passing. Even if they do not drive as well on the test as on previous lessons, he or she is still likely to pass, provided that there are no serious or dangerous errors. In any event, the extra training before taking the test will mean that these pupils are better prepared to drive unaccompanied after passing.

Fault assessment on its own will do little to improve the performance of learners. To benefit learners the following procedure should be adopted:

- Recognise the fault;
- Analyse the fault; and
- Correct the fault.

Fault recognition

Having recognised a fault, you should identify it as being minor, serious or dangerous. Minor faults can normally be corrected on the move. However, if a recurring pattern of minor faults is identified, you will need to spend some time on dealing with them before they become more serious.

Minor faults could include errors in coordination and inefficient or uneconomic driving style, slight inaccuracies in positioning (either travelling along the road or during the set manoeuvres) and harsh use of the controls.

Serious or dangerous faults will need to be discussed more fully. This discussion should be carried out while parked somewhere safe. Do not get into discussions at road junctions, or while pupils are trying to negotiate hazards – this will only confuse them which could lead to even more serious faults being made.

Fault analysis

When analysing faults you need to compare what your pupil is doing, or has done, with what you would be doing or would have done in similar circumstances.

Before analysing the fault you should give some general encouragement and feedback on any progress made before the fault occurred. This will make the pupil more receptive to the criticism which you are about to give. Another useful approach would be to ask the pupil: 'How do you think that drive/manoeuvre went?'

It may be that the pupil realises that a mistake has been made, in which case you could help them to analyse the fault for themselves.

Whichever method you use, you should:

- explain what was wrong (both the cause of the error and its effect and consequences);
- explain what should have happened; and
- explain why it is important (paying particular attention to how the error could affect other road-users).

Consider using a visual aid if you need to recreate a difficult situation or explain incorrect positioning on the road, or illustrate how other road-users were involved. Diagrams, models and magnetic boards are useful aids.

After analysing the fault, use your question and answer technique to make sure that the pupil has fully understood what went wrong, what should have happened, and why it is important. This will then lead to the last, and most important, part of the routine.

Fault correction

Remedial action will need to be offered while the fault and the improvements needed are still fresh in the pupil's mind. It is of little use to say that you will come back to the fault on the next lesson as by that time the pupil will have probably forgotten what to do.

If the fault involved the way in which the pupil dealt with a particular hazard or junction, the most effective way to correct it would be to get the pupil to approach the same situation again. Depending on the fault, you may decide to talk the pupil through the situation, or just prompt on the points which need improving. The main thing is that success is achieved. If time allows, a third approach to the same situation will help to validate your instruction, this time leaving the pupil to deal with it entirely unaided. Praise must be given when improvement has been made.

At the end of each lesson, you should ask yourself:

- Did I identify all the main faults made by my pupil?

- Did I correct all the minor faults on the move and stop to analyse the major faults as soon as convenient?

- Did I analyse the faults made with regard to what went wrong, what should have happened, and why it was important?

- Did I offer appropriate remedial action, bringing about improvement?

HAZARD PERCEPTION

Hazard perception is now part of the theory test for L drivers and is a subject that instructors need to be expert at – both in theory and practice.

The driving skills involved include:

- scanning the road well ahead;

- anticipating the actions and reactions of other road users;

- being aware of following traffic;

- planning an appropriate course of action;

- maintaining a safe and appropriate distance behind the vehicle in front;

- driving at a speed that is appropriate to the conditions.

However, the main element is CONCENTRATION!

As an instructor, your own perception of hazards is even more important. You should also be able to develop these skills in your learner drivers by utilising a variety of *practical teaching skills*, but mostly by effective 'Q and A' techniques.

A 'hazard' is usually defined as anything that might cause us to change our direction or to alter the speed of our vehicle. Some of these will be static hazards such as road junctions or bends; others might be moving hazards, such as pedestrians, cyclists, horse-riders, motorcyclists and other vehicles.

Using your 'Q and A' techniques you should be able to help your pupils to improve their skill in recognising and dealing with all types of hazard.

The ultimate aim of your instruction will be to enable your pupils to:

- scan the road ahead and behind effectively;
- anticipate the main points of danger;
- recognise that what we *can't* see is just as important as what we *can* see;
- think about what *might* happen as well as what *is* happening;
- give themselves time and space to carry out a particular manoeuvre or to avoid a problem;
- maintain absolute control of their vehicle while carrying out correct driving procedures.

Encouraging your pupils to look well ahead, keeping the eyes moving all the time and continually looking for clues as to what might happen, can achieve this.

EXPLANATION, DEMONSTRATION, PRACTICE

When teaching a skill as complex as driving a car, you must have clearly in mind all the component parts of the skill. Before attempting to teach the skill, you will need to ask:

1. What knowledge does the learner need in order to carry out the task successfully?

2. What attitudes should the learner have towards carrying out the task?

3. What manipulative and/or perceptive skills does the task involve?

Each component part of the skill will have a 'prepared' position from which the actual performance commences. This may involve positioning of the hands and/or feet and the use of the eyes in anticipation of carrying out the specific task. Being poised ready for action can be important from the point of view of smoothness, control, accuracy and safety.

For example, moving off requires the car to be in 'a prepared state': ie, gear selected, gas set, clutch to biting point, handbrake prepared. This will be followed by checking ahead, checking mirrors, checking blindspots, assessing whether it is safe to go and whether a signal is necessary, releasing the hand-brake, slowly bringing the clutch up and increasing the gas, and putting the hand back onto the steering wheel.

To help the learner to memorise this sequence, the following mnemonic could be used:

P (Prepare) – O (Observe) – M (Move)

An experienced driver gets into the car, starts up and moves off in a matter of seconds without having to think about it.

For the novice, things are not so simple. As the moving off procedure and the coordination of the clutch and gas is so vital for many other driving tasks, much practice will be needed to get it right.

With all these basic formative skills most pupils will benefit from a demonstration. It is all too easy for the instructor to assume that the pupil knows, understands, and can do what is required.

Prior to practising a new skill the learner should understand:

● WHY is has to be learnt;
● WHEN and WHERE it should be applied;
● WHAT is expected in learning the skill;
● HOW the skill is to be performed.

The most effective sequence of skill training is: 1) EXPLANATION, 2) DEMONSTRATION and 3) PRACTICE. This teaching routine is a prime example of how many of the PTS in this book can be brought together to form a strategy for learning.

Explanation

Briefings and explanations have been covered more fully in Chapter 3. The explanation should be tailored to take account of the level of ability of the learner. During the early stages of learning to drive, it might sometimes be better to concentrate on the KEY POINTS, so that the pupil is not OVERLOADED with information.

Once these key points are fully established it will be easier for the learner to understand and retain additional information given at a later date.

> *Most explanations will need to include the following: CONTROL (of the vehicle); OBSERVATIONS (hazard recognition, other road-users and response to them); and ACCURACY (positioning and steering of the vehicle).*

CONTROL – Briefings will need to cover control of the vehicle and speed approaching or dealing with hazards. This should include the manipulative aspects of driving; coordination of controls; smoothness; securing the vehicle when stationary.

OBSERVATIONS – This will contain necessary information on the LOOK, ASSESS, DECIDE routine; skills of perception; safety margins; attitudes towards other road-users.

ACCURACY – This section will cover aspects of steering; positioning and general accuracy; course and lane discipline where appropriate.

Any visual aids or diagrams that will clarify, reinforce or add authority to an explanation should be used. You will also find it useful to refer to the official DSA publications:

The Highway Code
Your Driving Test
Driving – the essential skills

These can be used to 'add weight to your words'.

Demonstration

A demonstration is useful in that the pupil will be able to see a model of correct behaviour which they can then imitate. Complex tasks can be broken down into component parts which can be demonstrated before the learner practises and repeats them until mastery is achieved. The advantages of you giving a demonstration are:

- you can adapt the demonstration to suit the specific needs of the pupil; and

- you are there to answer any questions which the pupil may wish to ask.

The demonstration must not be used to dazzle the learner with your own expertise. The key points in the preceding briefing or explanation should form an integral part of the demonstration by way of an abbreviated commentary.

A learner may often be genuinely unaware of a mistake. A demonstration will help to show them where they are going wrong and what is needed to correct the problem. This is especially so when the pupil's perception of safety margins; the need for 'holding back' procedures; and speed approaching hazards, is poor.

You might mention slowing down approaching a hazard and get no response from the learner if your pupil's understanding of 'slow' is different from your own. Under these circumstances a demonstration can be a valuable aid to you in persuading the pupil to modify what they are doing to fit in with how *you* want the manoeuvre carried out.

It may be helpful to pupils if you SIMULATE what they are doing so that they can appreciate the difference.

This technique would be particularly useful when giving feedback on the pupil's performance in the set manoeuvres.

Points to remember

1. Explain beforehand why you are going to demonstrate and what it is all about.

2. Pitch the demonstration and the commentary given while carrying it out to the correct level for the ability of the learner.

3. Make the demonstration as perfect an example as possible of what you want the pupil to do.

4. Restrict the commentary to key points only and those that are necessary for that particular learner.

5. Consolidate afterwards with a debriefing and controlled practice.

The demonstration should be concluded with a summary of the key points, which might then lead to a Q&A session to identify any aspects of the task which the learner still does not understand.

Practice

Having demonstrated the skill you should then allow your pupil to practice it as soon as possible. The first time the pupil attempts the skill, it is important that success is achieved.

There is nothing more demotivating for a learner than to watch you carry out a task perfectly and then to fail miserably trying to copy it. You could find that there is a need for prompting if the pupil is encountering difficulties or deviating from what they should be doing. For example, if the pupil is practising the turn in the road and not turning the wheel effectively, you may need to say: 'Use longer movements of the steering wheel and turn more briskly'.

Establishing good habits in these early stages while practising the manoeuvre will pay dividends for the learner later on.

When the pupil is practising new skills, check on the body language for signs of stress, frustration or despair. Be prepared to intervene if necessary. Encouragement and reassurance may be needed. Be prepared to change your lesson plan and go back to consolidating previously learnt skills to boost flagging confidence.

Controlled practice will allow the beginner to remain safe, and not be too unsympathetic to the vehicle. It involves the learner in following simple verbal instructions to carry out the component parts of the skill which, when brought together, form complete mastery.

The speed with which the learner interprets and responds to the instruction needs to be taken into account. This may vary from pupil to pupil. With some pupils it may be necessary to carry out tasks more slowly than normal.

The instructions given should eventually be reduced to prompting. As soon as the learner appears to be able to cope independently, the instruction should gradually be phased out.

The amount of prompting given will depend on the ability and willingness of learners to make decisions on their own. Some learners will require a lot of encouragement to act and think for themselves.

The ultimate objective is to get the learner to carry out each skill under all normal traffic conditions with no prompting from you at all.

Many learners complete their programme of training being able to carry out all the driving tasks required of them, but unable to do any of them particularly well. This is not helpful to the pupils, who may themselves feel that 'all is not well'.

The sequence of development should be:

- CONTROLLED PRACTICE;

- PROMPTED PRACTICE;

- TRANSFERRED RESPONSIBILITY;

- REFLECTION; then

- REVISION.

Prompting should not be necessary where the learner is about to be presented for the 'L' test!

After using the 'explain, demonstrate practise' (EDP) routine, you will need to ask yourself:

- Did I use the EDP routine to good effect?
- Did my briefing or explanations cover all the key points?
- Did my demonstration have the desired effect on the pupil?
- Did I assist my pupil to achieve initial success by prompting when necessary?
- Did I take account of the body language of the pupil when practising new skills?
- Am I flexible enough to change back to the pupil's previously learnt skills in order to boost confidence?
- Did I transfer responsibility as soon as it was appropriate to do so, or did I 'keep instructing' when it was no longer necessary?

PUPIL INVOLVEMENT

To help maintain the interest and attention of your pupil you need to bring the lesson to life, personalising it and making it enjoyable. At the end of any lesson your pupils should leave the car feeling not only that they have learnt something and achieved the objectives of the lesson, but also that they have enjoyed themselves.

A proportion of your pupils will probably come to you having had lessons with another instructor. Why is this? It is often because they feel they were not making progress with the previous instructor or were not enjoying the lessons.

Don't forget that each pupil is an individual. Use first names during the lesson and make eye contact when discussing things while stationary. Use the different speech elements we discussed in the previous chapter – metaphors, hyperbole and similes – to add interest and perhaps a touch of humour to the presentation.

Use visual aids when explaining things, and make sure that pupils can actually *see* what it is that you are showing them. So many instructors cover up what they are showing with their hands so pupils cannot see or understand the points being made!

Another way to make lessons more interesting for pupils is to INVOLVE them as much as possible by using the 'question and answer' technique. ('Q&A' is dealt with in more detail later in this chapter).

We have already talked about asking yourself questions to help you plan the lesson. Later in this chapter we will show you how to ask similar questions during the presentation to ensure that the pupil is participating.

VISUAL AIDS

A learning aid is any medium you might use to enable you to present your ideas, concepts, knowledge and skills in a manner that is more easily understood by your learner.

> *Learning aids can assist the learning process by helping to hold pupils' attention and generate an interest that stimulates the desire to learn.*

It has been said that, 'The purpose of a learning aid is to liberate the teacher from the limitations of his or her own speech'. But, while learning aids may help to make a good instructor even better, they will not compensate for bad teaching.

Learning aids range from a simple notepad and pencil to sophisticated driving simulators. Between these two extremes, there is a vast range of aids available to the instructor, many of which are visual. In this section we will concentrate on those aids of a visual nature that can be used in the car.

'A picture paints a thousand words' – provided it is a good picture! It is amazing how many instructors say to their pupils: 'I am not very good at drawing, but I am going to draw you a diagram to explain what I mean'.

The visual aids you use are limited only by your imagination. You can use your hands to explain how the clutch plates come together; you can use your fingers to show 'the thickness of a coin' when explaining the biting point; you can produce pre-prepared diagrams to assist you in explaining various aspects of road procedure, manoeuvres etc.

Be careful, however, not to overuse visual aids to the extent that they detract from the basic message you wish to put across.

Visual aids offer the following benefits:

- they add structure to your lesson;
- they provide a change of activity for the learner;
- they will assist you by reminding you what needs to be said;
- they will allow the pupil to recall and visualise previously encountered situations;
- they can help to clarify difficult concepts or show specific positions required when manoeuvring or dealing with hazards; and
- they stimulate the interest of the learner and help to maintain attention.

> *By being skilful in designing, creating and integrating visual aids in your presentation, you will be able to bring the lesson to life.*

When using visual aids in the car you should:

- avoid just reading from a script;
- talk to the pupil and not to the visual aid;
- turn the aid around so that the pupil can see it – it is for their benefit, not just for yours;
- avoid covering the visual aid with your hand – you may need to hold it with your right and use your left hand, or a pen, to point to the key parts;
- avoid 'pen-waving' because it can be threatening to the pupil; and
- once you have used the aid, put it away before it becomes a distraction.

The following ABC of visual aids used should be borne in mind:

ACCURACY – Try to ensure that the visual aid accurately recreates the situation you are trying to depict.
BREVITY – Keep drawings/diagrams simple and avoid having too many words or unnecessary detail.
CLARITY – Ensure that letters or words are big enough to be seen by the pupil.
DELETION – Use them then lose them, otherwise they become a distraction.
EMPHASIS – Make sure that the visual aid stresses the key points.

At the end of each lesson ask yourself:

- Did I take every opportunity to use visual aids in order to assist the learning process?
- Were the visual aids stimulating and effective?
- Did I identify any situations where a visual aid could have been useful? If so, should I think about designing one for future use?

QUESTION AND ANSWER TECHNIQUE

Of all the teaching tools available to you, the question and answer technique (Q&A) is probably the most useful. Using an effective Q&A technique can serve two major purposes:

- teaching understanding;
- testing understanding.

You will need to think carefully which use you have in mind before posing questions. More often than not you will need to use 'testing' questions at the start and at the end of the lessons, and 'teaching' questions during them.

At the start of lessons you should ask a few questions to test whether or not pupils remember what happened during the previous lesson. Pay particular attention to the 'successes' and 'achievements', especially if new skills were used and mastered.

Using questions at the start of lessons in this way will get pupils into the habit of answering them. This will make things easier for you when you get to the more important 'teaching' questions, which we cover in more detail later in this section.

Your purpose in using these 'teaching' questions is to motivate pupils by challenging or intriguing them and helping them to work out solutions and reasons for doing things by themselves.

There is nothing more frustrating than getting 'zero response' to your carefully thought out questions. Your pupils therefore need to be encouraged and conditioned to answering your questions.

At the end of lessons you can use 'testing' questions as a means of reminding pupils what took place during the drive and any improvements or achievements that have been made.

Asking appropriate questions while stationary and on the move will enable you to gain feedback on pupils' knowledge, understanding, experience and attitudes. Further questions can then help you to improve, alter or amend pupils' understanding.

As the larger part of the lessons (the exception being the 'Controls' lesson) will be on the move, it is the 'teaching' questions that will benefit pupils most.

The most important thing when using Q&A is that you ask the most suitable question for the situation you find yourself in!

Choosing appropriate questions

The questions you use must take account of the level of ability of the pupil and what is happening in the driving environment. Each drive will prompt a different set of questions. These may generally be broken down into two categories:

- what is happening or should be happening inside the vehicle;
- what is happening outside the vehicle, and how should the pupil be responding.

For pupils in the early stages of learning you are likely to need to ask 'in-car' questions concerning control, technique, smoothness, the use of mirrors and general observation.

With more advanced pupils, who should be able to control the vehicle in a reasonably safe, smooth manner, most of the questions will need to find out:

- whether they are aware of what is happening in front, behind and around the vehicle; and
- what action, if any, needs to be taken to deal with the situation, with safety in mind.

You will need to take account of:

- the pupil's ability;
- what is happening in the vehicle;
- what is happening outside the vehicle (ahead, behind and in the blind areas);
- the presence and actions of other road users;
- the weather conditions and visibility;
- road signs and markings.

Your job as an instructor is to read the road so far ahead, getting the 'big picture', so that you can anticipate what is likely to happen, leaving you enough time to ask the appropriate questions to get pupils involved in the decision-making process.

Some of the most important questions you ask should be designed to test pupils' hazard awareness. Remember that a hazard is anything around that may require you to alter your speed, change direction or stop.

With years of driving and instructional experience behind you, it is so easy to assume that your pupil will see and, more to the point, take the necessary action, to deal with hazards or other road users.

It is particularly important that your pupils are taught to respond to the more vulnerable road users – pedestrians (especially children and older people), cyclists and motorcyclists, people who may be disadvantaged by disability, a parent struggling to cross the road with a pram and toddlers.

In all of these cases, your vehicle may pose a threat to others. Your questions can help to ensure that pupils not only see the situation, but have the correct attitude to take the appropriate action to defuse it.

Some situations may arise where other vehicles pose a threat to yours – large lorries struggling to negotiate roundabouts, or swinging wide when turning into narrow entrances; buses stopping and moving off; dust-carts and skip lorries; goods vehicles making deliveries; emergency vehicles fighting to get through traffic; aggressive drivers who are in a hurry to get somewhere and may be setting the worst possible example.

Changes in the environment may also pose a threat – blind bends, narrow roads, poor surfaces, patchy mist or fog, sudden rain or snow, late summer sun low on the horizon, bright lights or oncoming headlights when driving after dark. Most of these hazards will require at the very least a reduction in speed.

As an instructor, you can capitalise on all these potentially dangerous situations by asking questions that will ensure that the pupil:

● has seen the hazard;

● has the correct attitude towards it and understands what action needs to be taken; and

● takes the appropriate action.

Of course, with pupils at any level there may occasionally be emergency situations which develop so fast that you have no time to start asking questions! In these circumstances, in the interests of safety, you have no alternative but to intervene.

After situations such as these, you can then put Q&A to good use by asking, 'Why do you think I took control then?'

The most effective questions are OPEN-ENDED QUESTIONS which need to be answered with some information rather than just a 'Yes' or 'No'. For example, if you ask a pupil if they have understood your explanations, the answer can only be 'Yes' or 'No'. This does not indicate whether the pupil has *actually* understood. You would, therefore, need to ask further questions in order to decide whether any learning had taken place.

Open-ended questions usually begin with the words: WHY, WHEN, HOW, WHO, WHERE, WHAT and WHICH.

The weakest of these is WHICH because this could be answered with a guess. You would then need to ask another question to find out if the pupil had simply guessed correctly.

The most powerful teaching word is WHY. For example, if you asked your pupil which signs are the most important, round ones or triangular ones and the pupil answered, 'Round ones' you would then need to ask the question, 'Why are round signs more important than triangular ones?' It would have been better to have asked that question in the first place.

You should always try to ask a question which will give you the answer that you are looking for. The idea is not to baffle pupils but to help them to work things out for themselves.

Open-ended questions can be used on the move to test a pupil's awareness of approaching hazards and what action should be taken. However, they should not require lengthy answers or a discussion. You can sometimes ask two questions at once – for example, 'What does this sign mean and how are you going to deal with it?'

Questions which require a long answer or a discussion should only be used when parked at the roadside somewhere safe and convenient.

Avoid asking questions while a pupil is trying to negotiate a junction or other hazard. This may confuse them and could result in a loss of concentration, leading to further driving errors.

The skill of the instructor is to choose questions wisely to get the pupil thinking and involved in decision making.

You should always confirm your pupils' understanding of what has been explained by careful use of the question and answer technique. Think about how you phrase the question:

● use simple wording that can be easily understood; and

● make sure the questions are answerable and reasonable.

It is no good posing a question which could be answered with any number of replies. Do not use trick questions which will only undermine the confidence of the pupil, make them feel foolish and defeat the objective of the question.

Most driving instructors are very good at telling their pupils what to do and how to do it, but very few ensure that learning and understanding have taken place by skilful use of the question and answer technique. As well as using questions yourself, invite questions from your pupil – 'Is there anything you are not sure about?'

Never ASSUME that your pupil has understood everything you have said!

As in all things, PRACTICE MAKES PERFECT and you will find that the more you use the Q&A technique, the more accomplished you will become. After a while you will build up an armoury of questions designed to suit most pupils and most situations.

Never assume that pupils will see and interpret things in the same way that you do. When a difference of opinion does occur, you may have to ask more searching questions, perhaps while stationary, until you can persuade pupils to see things in the way that you see them.

Remember that the benefits of doing things 'your way' usually include:

- improved safety;
- more smoothness;
- less effort involved and greater efficiency;
- cost savings through more economy or less wear and tear.

Give plenty of praise (positive reinforcement) when questions are answered well, even if they may only be partly answered. In this case you could rephrase the answer, filling in the gaps and thus making it complete.

Do not be disparaging or sarcastic about incorrect answers, otherwise pupils may 'clam up' and be reluctant to answer future questions.

Until it comes naturally to you, try asking yourself questions when you are driving alone. This is very similar to the technique used by police drivers of 'giving a commentary' but more productive for driving instructors in that it will help you to improve your Q&A technique, thus making lessons more effective both for you and for your pupils.

Always give pupils time to answer questions. Never ask another question until the first one has been answered. Be careful not to bombard them with questions or turn lessons into 'interrogations'. If necessary, find somewhere safe to stop so that you can discuss a pupil's response to questions.

During every drive there will be situations on which you can base your questions. These questions will help pupils to see things as you see them, stand them in good stead once they have passed the test and help them to achieve 'safe driving for life'.

Once you have become skilled at using Q&A, don't forget that, as pupils near test standard, you should be reducing the number of questions you are using. By this stage you should have transferred responsibility so that pupils are making their own decisions without help from you. The problem with many instructors is that once they get proficient at asking questions, they don't know when to stop – so don't get bogged down with asking irrelevant ones.

If you still need to ask questions in the last few lessons leading up to the test, you should ask yourself the one final question – 'Should this pupil be taking the test at all?'

> *At the end of each lesson, when analysing your own performace, ask yourself whether the questions you used during the lesson achieved their objectives.*

INTERVENTION

Some learner drivers may fail to recognise potentially dangerous traffic situations in time to employ the necessary procedure or defensive strategy.

> *Instructors must read the road well ahead. They must also learn to anticipate a learner's incorrect response to situations and be prepared to compensate for it, either by verbal or physical action.*

When giving driving lessons you must maintain a safe learning environment for your pupils by:

- planning routes commensurate with their ability;

- forward planning and concentrating on the overall traffic situation – front, rear and to the sides;

- being alert and anticipating learners' incorrect actions or lack of activity in difficult situations;

- giving clear instructions in good time for them to respond;

- overriding learners' decisions when necessary; and

- being prepared to intervene verbally or physically.

Many learners show a reluctance to slow down, give way, stop, or hold back when necessary. This is usually because they have an innate fear of stopping. If they stop, they know they then have to get the car moving again – one of the most difficult things for learners to do in the early stages!

This reluctance to deal with hazards defensively may cause the situation to develop into an emergency. Where the situation is allowed to reach this critical level, there are two possible unwanted reactions: (1) the pupil may do nothing and remain frozen at the controls or (2) they may over-react at the last moment, resulting in harsh, uncontrolled braking, the effect of which is difficult to predict.

It is in situations like this that expert instructors prove their worth. By intervening, either verbally or physically, a possible accident situation can be avoided.

There are four main reasons why you should intervene:

1. To prevent risk of injury or damage to persons or property (including the driving school car).

2. To prevent the pupil from breaking the law which could lead to you being prosecuted for 'aiding and abetting'.

3. To prevent excessive stress to the learner in certain unplanned circumstances (for example, an emergency situation).

4. To prevent mechanical damage to the vehicle (for example, in the event of an injudicious gear change).

Because intervention can undermine confidence and inhibit the progress of the learner, it should be kept to a minimum. Verbal intervention should, if time allows, be used before considering the use of physical intervention or the dual controls.

Verbal intervention

A verbal instruction or command will usually be successful in dealing with most traffic situations or driver errors, providing it is given early enough.

Verbal instructions and memory prompts will be used more frequently in the early stages of learning to drive, and may take the form of more specific instructions such as: 'Use the mirrors *well* before…', 'More brake!', 'Ease off the brake' and 'Clutch down'.

These more positive commands will often be needed to make sure that your pupil slows down early enough on the approach to a potential hazard.

'Hold back!', 'Give way!' and 'Wait!' are other examples of *positive* instructions which require a *positive* response or reaction from the pupil, but which also leave some freedom of judgement.

When using this type of command, the pitch and tone of your voice should be used to convey the degree of urgency to the pupil.

The use of the word 'Stop' should generally be restricted to those occasions when other instructions have not been followed by the pupil or when the pupil has not responded positively. Incorrect use of this command could mean that your pupil over-reacts and stops too suddenly or in an unsuitable position. Unnecessary and too frequent use of the word 'Stop' – for example, when parking – could have the effect that pupils will not respond quickly enough in urgent situations.

Physical intervention

Use of any form of physical intervention, or the dual controls, should be restricted to situations when the verbal instruction has not been followed or there is insufficient time for it to be given or acted on.

In these situations, you may need to consider the main alternatives:

- use of the dual brake and/or clutch; or
- assistance with the steering.

Using the dual brake/clutch

The following points need to be considered:

- Avoid sitting with your legs crossed when teaching. When approaching hazards, keep your right foot discreetly near the dual brake but not riding on it.
- Avoid unnecessary or 'fidgety' movements of your feet as this may unnerve your pupil.
- Only use the dual clutch when it is absolutely necessary and *never* to 'make things easy' for the pupil.
- Make effective use of the dual mirror before using the dual brake.
- If your pupil has 'frozen' on the gas pedal, avoid using the dual clutch as this could cause a blown head gasket.
- Give the pupil time to use the brake before intervening. If you both use the brake at the same time, this could cause problems.
- Consider using the dual brake to help you to 'buy time' if you have to help with the steering. This applies particularly where the pupil may be trying to turn a corner too fast.

Assistance with steering

This should only be used to make slight alterations to road position. It would be better for you to tell the pupil to 'Steer to the right' or 'Steer to the left'.

Bear in mind the following points:

- Minor corrections with steering are usually more practical and safer alternatives to using the dual brake.
- Use only your right hand when assisting with steering.

- Avoid physical contact. If you get hold of the pupil's hand or arm and they let go of the wheel, you have lost control.

- If you wish to steer to the left, hold the wheel near the top so that you can 'pull down'.

- If you wish to steer to the right, hold the wheel near the bottom so that you can 'push up'.

- If the situation is such that more drastic turning of the wheel is required, it would be safer and much less worrying for the pupil if you used the dual brake.

- Never get into a fight with the pupil over the wheel – you might lose!

There may be occasions when assistance with both steering and braking are required. For example, it may be essential to hold the steering wheel while using the dual brake to prevent the pupil from oversteering. In order to gain more time, you may need to reduce and control the speed of the vehicle with the dual brake, particularly when the pupil has 'frozen' on the gas pedal.

In any potentially dangerous situation, you will need to use your experience to decide which method of intervention is required. You may need to use the dual clutch at the same time as manipulating the gear lever to prevent an inappropriate gear change. This will allow your pupil to concentrate on maintaining the correct speed and position.

Examples of other types of physical intervention which do crop up from time to time are:

- selecting a missed gear at a critical time or place;

- preventing an incorrect gear selection by 'covering the gear lever' until the correct speed is reached;

- covering the dual clutch so as to be ready to prevent the car moving off at an inappropriate time;

- rectifying an error with the handbrake when there is no time to tell the pupil to do so;

- switching off the engine to prevent mechanical damage;

- cancelling an injudicious signal with safety in mind when there is no time to tell the pupil to do so.

The need for any kind of intervention can be kept to an absolute minimum by careful route planning and matching the road and traffic conditions to the ability of the pupil.

You may encounter some resentment against any form of physical interference or the use of the dual controls. This could result in the pupil losing confidence in themselves and in you as a teacher. You should therefore make sure that:

- you do not get into the habit of using physical intervention or the dual controls excessively or unnecessarily;
- having used any physical intervention, you fully explain to the pupil WHAT you did to control the car, and WHY it was necessary to do it!

SELLING IDEAS AND CONCEPTS

In driving instruction, selling skills go far beyond being able to persuade potential pupils to book driving lessons with your school.

Development of your Practical Teaching Skills will enable you to become more effective in selling ideas and concepts to your pupils when you are teaching in the car on a one-to-one basis. In this section we are going to concentrate on this aspect of selling.

Everybody has sold something at some time in their lives, and everybody is involved with selling whether they realise it or not.

Selling in the car is much more informal than selling generally. Although simple instinct will help you when selling ideas, the development and controlled use of many of the communication skills will improve your ability to convince others that they should 'buy' your ideas and concepts, as well as your driving lessons.

> *Remember that as a good, effective instructor you need to be able to persuade pupils to do what you want them to do, in the way that you want them to do it!*

When selling informally on a one-to-one basis, if you are skilful, you will involve the pupil in what is happening by explaining the benefits of following your advice and doing things your way, and listening to the response.

When selling ideas or concepts, you must be as knowledgeable as possible about the issue under discussion and you will need to make good use of your communication skills, especially:

- your verbal communication skills;
- your listening skills; and
- your use of positive body language and the interpretation of the body language of your pupils.

When selling ideas you first of all need to explain WHAT it is that you require your pupil to do or understand; second comes HOW you want whatever is being done to be carried out and, third, WHY it is important that it is carried out in a particular way.

The most important of these is WHY. There is no point in pupils knowing WHAT is supposed to be done if they don't know WHY it needs to be done in a particular way.

The skilful, and two-way, use of the question and answer technique will help you to achieve all three objectives.

> *The good instructor will help pupils to arrive at their own conclusions for themselves by guiding the discussion.*

As in selling services, any objections should be dealt with by further questioning and explanation so it is very important that you listen carefully to everything your pupil says. You must try to draw them into the discussion rather than give a lecture.

When sat at the side of the road or in the classroom, the body language you use when selling ideas must be positive and support and endorse what you are saying. For example:

- forceful hand gestures may be used to emphasise important points;

- strong eye contact should be made to show your sincerity and belief in what you are saying; and

- nods of approval coupled with smiles should be given when the pupil reaches good conclusions – this will encourage the pupil to participate further.

You should watch carefully the body language of pupil's to help you identify any resistance to your ideas or concepts.

If such resistance is detected, question them: 'You don't seem very happy with that. What's the problem?'

Once you have identified the problem, you should handle it like any other objection, outlining the benefits of doing things or seeing things your way. Don't forget the benefits will nearly always relate to SAFETY, CONVENIENCE and COST SAVINGS.

For example, you might be trying to convince a pupil that she really doesn't have to signal every time she moves off when there is no other road-user in sight.

The debriefing might go something like this:

'OK Julie, how do you think that drive went?'

'Well, I don't think it was too bad. I know I was a bit jerky with the clutch when I moved off.'

'Yes, it was a little bit jerky but we can always work on that and it will get better with practice. I liked the way you waited for the red car coming from behind to pass before you moved off, but do you really think you needed to signal?'

'Well my Dad said it's always best to signal just in case.'

'Yes I agree that if it had been a busy High Street a signal might have been a good idea, but you did check your blind spot again and nothing was coming, and there was no oncoming traffic. I had a pupil on the test the other week and the examiner stopped her on a busy road to give his next instruction. Before moving off again, the pupil checked her mirror, saw a bus coming along so decided to give a signal for moving off. The bus driver realised the learner might have been on test and decided to stop for her. The pupil then got confused and didn't know whether to go or wait. In the meantime the bus driver got fed up with waiting and started to move off again. At the same time, the pupil decided to move off and the examiner had to intervene. If the pupil had assessed the situation correctly and not signalled there wouldn't have been a problem would there? If there was a bus coming you wouldn't move off in any case would you?'

'No, not really!'

'Good. Well let's try moving off again. This time I'd like you to assess the situation yourself, and then decide if you need to signal. Try to get used to assessing situations and making decisions based on safety.'

At the end of each lesson where you have had to sell ideas or concepts to your pupils, analyse your own performance by asking yourself: 'Have I used my selling skills to good effect, and successfully convinced my pupil WHY it is important that they do things my way?'

5

The ADI Part 1 exam

The purpose of this book is to improve your practical teaching skills. It is therefore not our intention to cover in detail information that you will find in the other reading materials recommended by the DSA for this test.

We are including this short chapter to ensure that you are aware of the wide range of knowledge and understanding you will need for the Part 1; and to emphasise that this will also give you a good grounding for the practical elements of the ADI exam – and, of course, for your future as a driving instructor.

THE SYLLABUS

The subjects covered are:

- The principles of road safety.
- The techniques of driving a car correctly.
- The theory and practice of learning, teaching and assessment.
- The tuition required to teach pupils how to drive a car.
- The Highway Code.
- The DSA publications.
- Interpretation of the reasons for test failure.
- Knowledge for the needs of driving instruction.

All of the questions taken from the syllabus have been grouped into ten subject areas and these are grouped into four main categories as follows:

- Road procedure.
- Traffic signs and signals; car control; pedestrians; mechanical knowledge.
- Driving test; disabilities; law.
- Publications; instructional techniques.

To prepare yourself properly for all three parts of the exam you need a thorough knowledge of the following publications and forms:

- *Driving – the essential skills*, ISBN 0-11-552224-7;
- *The Highway Code*, ISBN 0-11-552290-5;
- *Know Your Traffic Signs*, ISBN 0-11-551612-3;
- *The Official Driving Test*, ISBN 0-11-552254-9;
- *The Driving Instructor's Handbook*, ISBN 0-7494-3085-0;
- *The Advanced Driver's Handbook*, ISBN 0-7494-1501-0;
- *The Official DSA Theory Test Guide for Car Drivers and Motorcycles*, ISBN 0-11-552196-8;
- *The Official DSA Guide for Driving Instructors*, ISBN 0-11-551785-5;
- *The Official Guide to Accompanying Learner Drivers*, ISBN 0-11-552178-X;
- *The Motor Vehicles (Driving Licences) Regulations 1999*, ISBN 0-11-085390-3;
- DL25A/B – *Driving Test Report Form* – you will find this reproduced in *The Driving Instructor's Handbook*;
- *D100 Leaflet – What you need to know about driving licences*, published by DVLA and available from them or any main post office;
- *V100 Leaflet – Registering and licensing your motor vehicle*, published by DVLA and available from them or any main post office;
- *D1 Application for a driving licence*, published by DVLA and available from them or any main post office;
- ADI26/PT Forms 1–10 – you will find these reproduced and explained in Chapter 6 of this book, 'Preparing for the Test of Instructional Ability';
- *And the book you are now reading.*

As you can see, this list is quite extensive and covers a wide range of subject knowledge.

> *Do not fall into the trap of believing that you will be able to memorise the question bank by rote learning.*

For one thing, there are over 900 questions in the official bank and, because they are computer-generated, the papers vary. Secondly, some of the questions are designed to test your understanding – not just your memory.

Remember, you are not only preparing for the theory test. You will also need an understanding of the principles involved in safe and effective driving for the Part 2 test; and also those involved in good teaching practices to prepare you for the test of instructional ability.

DEVELOPING STUDY SKILLS

In preparation for the ADI Part 1 test, you will need to develop your study skills so that your learning is effective. This will be even more important if it is a long time since you were studying for any sort of theory test. Developing your own study skills should also stand you in good stead later, should you wish to take further qualifications in your quest for personal development.

Some of your learners, too, will need advice when organising their studies for the theory part of the L test.

In developing these study skills, you will need to:

- make time available;
- find the right place to study; and
- formulate a study plan.

ORGANISING YOUR STUDIES

If you feel there are too many distractions at home and you enrol on an intensive classroom course, because of the volume of the subject matter you will still have to spend quite a lot of your private time studying.

You need to organise your study time so that learning is maximised. This means fitting it in around your other commitments and in a quiet place where you will be able to concentrate properly.

Making time available

Depending on how quickly you want to progress through your course, you may need to consider putting on hold for a while some of your social activities. However, so that you don't become bored or overloaded with studying, you will need to establish a balance that will allow you to still enjoy some free time while maximising your learning.

You will need to consider the impact of this study period on your close relatives. Try not to let yourself become so involved that they become resentful. This will only cause personal stress for everyone, and this, in turn, will affect your learning rate. You could try to get them involved by asking them to test you. This may even benefit them by updating their knowledge of the Highway Code rules and other information.

Time management is crucial. Whenever possible try to arrange your studies to fit in with the times when you know you will be in the best frame of mind to concentrate. You may have to experiment by studying at different times of the day.

The key ingredients to successful studying are:

- *Motivation;*
- *Self-discipline; and*
- *Determination.*

Finding the right place to study

Being in the right place is just as important as studying at the best time. The quality of your learning will be enhanced dramatically if the environment you choose is 'conducive to learning'.

Some types of learning, for example 'learning by rote', require a quiet environment that is free from distractions. Rote learning is where you are learning things by memory, for example, the tables of stopping distances.

Whatever the type of learning, you still need a relatively quiet environment. Provided that those sharing your home understand and respect your needs, you will probably be able to 'shut yourself away' without creating too much disturbance.

As this course involves such a large amount of reference material, you will need lots of space in which to spread your books around. You should try to get yourself properly organised with these and some writing materials before you start each session.

Some people like a little background music, but noise should be kept to a minimum as it can be a distraction and cause you to lose concentration.

Having established the time and place for your studies, you now have to ensure that you have a properly organised study plan.

Formulating a study plan

Studying is another skill that, like other skills, will improve with practice, determination and a planned approach.

Everyone is different. Some people are naturally studious and content to spend hours at a time studying and reading. Others find it not so easy – especially if they have not been in a learning environment since leaving school.

Remember, you may have to accept that some of your other activities are going to have to be shelved so that you can concentrate fully. To help maximise the quality of your studies, you need to formulate a plan. Try the following:

- Set personal objectives that you should be able to achieve within the time you set for them.

- Decide how much time you will need to set aside each day/week in order to achieve the deadline you set for yourself. You may need advice from your course provider on how long preparation for the theory test is likely to take you.

- Formulate a timetable on which you can set targets for completing each specific module of the syllabus.

- Try to organise the material so that you are reading about similar subjects in one study session.

- Make sure that your timetable is not too restrictive by including some relaxation time between study periods. Leave yourself at least one whole day a week; and one or two study-free weeks if you are finding the course a bit 'heavy-going'.

- Monitor your progress to ensure that you are not falling behind.

- Try not to become despondent if you feel you are falling behind and ask yourself if you are able to devote a little more time to the work.

- Don't panic, as this would only lead to stress and would do nothing for your learning process. Discuss your problems with your course provider, other trainees, close relatives or friends.

- If the pressures are too great, then it is better to consider revising your timetable. It would be better to delay taking the test than to take it before you have a thorough understanding of the course materials.

- Never let a study programme get on top of you but *KEEP ON TOP OF IT*!

The foregoing list should help, when you have qualified as a driving instructor, in advising your pupils on how to study effectively for their theory test.

As the ADI test covers such a wide range of subject knowledge, you need to properly organise your studies so that in any one session you are reading about related topics. This will prevent your suffering from an overload of mixed information that can often end up with nothing being remembered.

A fully structured programme is available from Margaret Stacey. Banded into separate workbooks, this material is now widely used by training organisations throughout the UK. You will find the necessary information on Margaret's Web site – www.autodriva.co.uk Alternatively, you can contact her by phone, fax or post – details are given at the front of this book.

The ADI theory test is taken at most 'L' driver theory centres and therefore appointments are quite readily available. Before applying for your test, you should feel confident that you have carefully studied all of the recommended materials and that you have a thorough understanding of all of the rules, regulations and teaching principles involved in driving and driving instruction.

ON THE DAY OF THE TEST

Allow plenty of time to get to the test centre with a few minutes to spare. Remember, these days you cannot predict how long a journey will take. If you are late, you will become stressed. Hardly the right frame of mind for concentration!

Take with you the appointment confirmation and your driving licence. If you do not have a photocard licence, you will also need some sort of photographic identification, such as your passport.

The test is computer-based with one question at a time being shown on the screen. Whether or not you are familiar with computer usage, you will be given a few minutes' practice.

The test paper will have 100 questions, each with a choice of four answers, only one of which is correct. Read each question very carefully at least twice. It may sometimes be easy to eliminate an obviously incorrect answer, but the choices remaining may be very similar. Some questions will even expect you to remember exact wording from the reading materials. This is why your study and understanding of the textbooks is so important.

If you're unsure about any questions, the computer system allows you to go backwards and forwards through them and to change your answers. If you're really not sure about one, it's better to tick the answer you think is the most appropriate. After all, you won't lose any more marks with a wrong answer than you would have by not having answered it.

You are allowed an hour and a half to complete the test. Make good use of any time left to re-check your answers. Don't be distracted when you see others leaving after only a short while. As well as other ADI candidates, there will also be learners taking their theory test and they have far fewer questions to answer. Anyway, the trainee instructors may have given up because they didn't study properly!

The result will be given to you before you leave the test centre. When you pass, you will also receive an application for the driving ability test. If you fail, you will be given an application for a further attempt.

6

The ADI Part 2 exam

Although this chapter deals in detail with the ADI test of driving ability, you should be teaching your pupils to drive to a similar style as that required of you.

It is accepted that although new drivers preparing for the L test can't be expected to drive at the same standard as you, they should be taught the same syllabus – that is, a syllabus that will result in 'safe driving for life'.

As you read through this chapter, therefore, you should consider how you will structure your courses to ensure that, as far as possible, you apply a similar set of criteria when teaching drivers at all levels of ability.

The major difference will be in how you will be assessed and how your learner drivers are assessed.

For this part of the exam your personal driving skills must be of a very high standard. You should not be trying to drive merely as a very good learner – the test is much more stringent than that.

The DSA expects you to show that you have a thorough understanding of safe and effective driving techniques; and that you are able to demonstrate these skills efficiently. In particular, you must be able to put into practice all of the following subjects:

- expert handling of the controls;
- application of correct road procedures;
- anticipating the actions of other road users and taking appropriate action;
- sound judgement of distance, speed and timing;
- consideration for the convenience and safety of other road users;

- moving away straight ahead and at an angle;
- overtaking, meeting or crossing the path of other vehicles, and taking an appropriate course without undue hesitancy;
- turning left- and right-hand corners correctly and without undue hesitancy;
- stopping the vehicle as in an emergency safely and under full control;
- reversing into limited openings to the left and right;
- reverse parking behind a parked vehicle;
- turning the vehicle to face the opposite direction using forward and reverse gears.

During the test you should endeavour to drive as normally as possible. In other words, don't try to 'put on an act' for the benefit of your examiner. The examiner would undoubtedly see through this and, anyway, you would probably not be able to keep the 'act' going for the duration of the test. It could also distract you, taking away your concentration from what's happening around you.

As with the practical L test, the examiner will explain a few of the 'ground rules' before you start the test. These will normally include:

- 'Follow the road ahead unless I give you an instruction to turn off.'
- 'I will tell you in good time if we are going to turn to the left or the right at a junction.'
- 'If you are unclear about any of my instructions, don't be afraid to ask – they will then be repeated or clarified.'
- 'Drive as you normally would – but remember that a high standard of competence is required.'

As well as driving over a varied route incorporating different types of road and traffic conditions, the test will include, if practicable, all of the following manoeuvres:

- up- and down-hill starts;
- emergency stop;
- left and right reverse;
- reverse parking;
- turning in the road.

During the test the examiner will be looking in detail at all aspects of your driving under two main headings – *control of the vehicle* and *road procedures*.

CONTROL

Take proper precautions before starting the engine

In the normal way check that the handbrake is on and that the gear lever is in neutral before starting the engine. (If you are a candidate with a disability and taking the test in a car with automatic transmission, select the 'N' or 'P' position.)

In some situations, for example in heavy traffic conditions, it is perfectly permissible to restart the engine in first gear, so long as the clutch is disengaged.

Make proper use of accelerator, clutch, gears, footbrake, handbrake, steering

The *foot controls* should be used progressively and smoothly without any harsh or jerky movements. Push gently on the *footbrake* to begin with and then press a little harder as the brakes start to work. Ease off the pedal just before the car comes to a standstill to achieve a smooth stop.

The *clutch* should be used only in conjunction with a gear change, just before stopping or carrying out a low-speed manoeuvre. At all other times, make sure that the clutch is engaged, particularly in between gear changes; and that your foot is completely off the pedal.

Use the *handbrake* if you are going to be stationary for any length of time or if the car is on a slope. Use it only when the car has stopped, but don't assume that it is necessary to apply it every time you are stationary.

Using the gears

Because modern braking systems and gearboxes are so efficient and reliable, it is not usually necessary to change down progressively through each of the gears. You should normally slow the car down by using the brakes and then select the appropriate gear for the hazard. This gives you more time to concentrate on your speed, position and observations of other traffic. It also enables you to keep both hands on the steering wheel. Remember, the weight of the car is thrown forwards during braking. Using the brakes to slow down means that you are less likely to wear out the more expensive parts of the car, ie the clutch, gearbox and transmission.

Steering

For normal driving use the pull/push method of steering, avoiding crossing your hands on the wheel. However, at very low manoeuvring speeds, particularly when reversing, it is acceptable (and often preferable) to use a 'hand-over-hand' method.

One-handed steering is useful when reversing on a straight course as it enables you to turn in the seat with the right hand at the top of the wheel and the left on the back of the seat. Whichever method you are using, make sure that you don't let the wheel slip when straightening up. At normal driving speeds hold the wheel at 'quarter to three' or 'ten to two' with a light grip. You only need a firmer grip when turning. Look well ahead to maintain a smooth and steady course.

Move away safely and under control

Check all mirrors and blind areas before moving off. Remember these latter checks are to cover those areas to the sides and rear of your car not seen in the mirrors. You are checking, for example, for traffic emerging from side roads and driveways, and cyclists or pedestrians crossing the road diagonally behind you.

Use a signal if you think that other road users, including cyclists and pedestrians, would benefit. Coordinate the use of hand and foot controls, steering, clutch and handbrake to achieve smooth and controlled starts. On downhill starts use the footbrake and the clutch effectively to avoid 'coasting'.

Stop the vehicle in an emergency promptly and under control

You will normally be expected to carry out this manoeuvre at a speed of about 40 mph. From your knowledge of braking distances, you should appreciate that it is going to take four times the distance to stop than when travelling at 20 mph.

You must react promptly. Keep both hands on the steering wheel while braking to maintain full control of your position. Remember that most of the weight of the car is thrown forwards onto the front wheels, making the steering heavier.

Use the footbrake firmly and progressively. If the front wheels lock, release the brake pressure momentarily and reapply firm pressure. Once the car has stopped secure it. Before moving away again, make sure you make the appropriate observations all round – including checking the nearside and offside.

Reversing to the left – under control, with proper observations, with reasonable accuracy

Carry out the manoeuvre slowly so that you have plenty of time for all-round observations throughout the exercise. This also allows time for smooth and unhurried control of the car. At the start of the manoeuvre check all round, particularly in the blind area over your right shoulder. While reversing, keep checking all round for approaching traffic and for any pedestrians who may be crossing the road. If traffic approaches the junction from the road you are reversing into, be ready to pull forward and restart the exercise.

With any of the manoeuvre exercises, the observations are as important as the control skills. Make sure you respond correctly to others, waiting for them when appropriate.

Reversing to the right – under control, with proper observations, with reasonable accuracy

This exercise is really two separate manoeuvres.

When you are moving over to the right-hand side of the road make sure that you use the mirrors effectively and avoid getting in the way of vehicles turning in and out of the side road as well as oncoming traffic. Use signals correctly and position the car so that other road users will see what your intentions are.

During the reverse part of the manoeuvre, your all-round observations are even more important because the car is on the wrong side of the road, in the path of any oncoming vehicles. When you have turned in, look down the road over your right shoulder, but with regular glances to the front and side.

Remember to respond to other road users correctly.

Reverse parking – under control, with proper observations, with reasonable accuracy

Although you would normally carry out this manoeuvre into a space between two parked cars, on the test candidates are usually asked to complete it within a gap of about two car lengths and with only the leading vehicle there.

Take a note of any gradients and maintain full control throughout. As you are reversing against the traffic flow, all-round observation is essential. Remember that the front of the car will swing out as you start to turn, so check for traffic and pedestrians in that area. You will also need to be aware of pedestrians who may be crossing and to respond accordingly.

If another vehicle stops close behind you, it may be necessary to move on and start again in a different location. Using your reversing and/or brake lights as appropriate might help to warn other drivers of your intentions.

Turning in the road – under control, with proper observations, with reasonable accuracy

Select a suitable place for the manoeuvre, avoiding obstructions, driveways and entrances. Be aware of any street furniture or exceptionally high kerbs that might affect your positioning.

Keep the vehicle moving very slowly whilst turning the steering briskly. Apply '*opposite lock*' as appropriate towards the end of each part of the manoeuvre.

Maintain all-round observations on each section of the exercise. As your vehicle is obstructing the road, give way to approaching traffic. But make sure that you respond appropriately to other drivers' actions and complete the manoeuvre promptly if it is clear or if another road user is waiting for you. You can usually judge this situation by making eye contact with the other driver and by the positioning of the other car.

ROAD PROCEDURE

Make effective use of the mirrors well before signalling, changing direction, overtaking

'*Effective use*' means not only looking, but also taking note of what is happening. This then helps you to make the correct decisions about how your intended actions are likely to affect any following drivers.

'*Well before*': on the approach to hazards, make sure that you use the mirrors early and effectively. This will give you time to work out how far behind and how fast following drivers may be before you take any action.

'*Signalling, changing direction, overtaking*': By using the mirrors effectively and in good time you will be able to decide whether to give a signal in any particular situation and then time the signal correctly and as appropriate.

As long as you are using the mirrors consistently and effectively *before* slowing down, speeding up, changing lanes, stopping, positioning, turning, moving out, etc., you will know exactly what's happening around you at all times. There is then no need to think in terms of 'I need to look in the mirrors every few seconds.'

Give signals by direction indicator/by arm – where necessary, correctly, properly timed

If you are using the mirrors effectively, you will be constantly aware of other road users around you. You need to take this into account when assessing whether a signal would be appropriate and also when to time it.

Use a signal if you feel that it would help or inform any other road user, but avoid unnecessary or indiscriminate signals. For example, giving a signal to pass a parked vehicle where there is a turning on the right might give the wrong impression. Signalling left after overtaking a moving vehicle might lead the other driver to think that you are going to turn left or that you intend to stop.

If you *are* going to signal, make sure that you use the correct one and that it is given in good time for others to take the appropriate action. The timing of your signals is important. For example, when preparing to turn right off a dual carriageway where faster moving traffic is overtaking you, your signal should be delayed so as not to confuse the overtaking drivers, but it should be given early enough to warn any following drivers.

Take prompt and appropriate actions at all traffic signs, road markings, traffic lights, signals by traffic controllers, other road users

You should be constantly scanning the road ahead for all types of road markings and signs. By doing this you can often anticipate what might happen as well as seeing the more obvious situations where you are obliged to do something.

A simple example would be a set of traffic lights where green has been showing for some time. In this situation, you can anticipate that the light will probably change and prepare to 'take prompt and appropriate action'. Similarly, you can anticipate the probability of a red light changing and be able to time your approach more efficiently and effectively.

On the approach to complex multi-lane junctions and roundabouts be aware of the directional signs and road markings. Plan ahead and decide early on your positioning and lane selection, and make sure that you maintain lane discipline through the hazard.

Remember that you are in the middle of a moving traffic situation, sharing the road space with others who can sometimes be unpredictable.

Exercise proper care in the use of speed

Apart from the obvious need to recognise and comply with speed limits, there are many situations in which you need to reduce your speed to allow for the conditions.

A speed limit is the *maximum* speed permissible for that particular road and not a target to aim at. Although you will be expected to keep up a reasonable speed where possible, there are many times when you need to drive at lower speeds. You need to allow for what is happening around you in terms of traffic movements and also for what *might* happen – near entrances; in residential areas; and close to schools or playgrounds.

Make progress by driving at a speed appropriate to the road and traffic conditions avoiding undue hesitancy

This section includes driving at an appropriate speed at all times, ie without unnecessarily holding up other traffic or by travelling too slowly in areas where there is a higher speed limit and the conditions are suitable.

At road junctions and roundabouts take appropriate opportunities to proceed by adjusting your speed and by timing the approach so as to avoid stopping unnecessarily. Remember that on the approach to a roundabout you need to keep looking to the right for suitable gaps in the traffic while also keeping a check on what is happening in front of you. Too often drivers on a driving test stop at junctions, simply because they feel that this conforms to the examiner's expectations. Another major cause of hesitancy at junctions is when drivers concentrate only on the approaching traffic, rather than on judging the available gaps.

Keep a safe distance behind vehicles

By applying the 'two-second' rule, you should find that you are always in a position to be able to stop safely in good time and to take appropriate action in response to other traffic.

If you are being followed too closely, your separation distance should be increased to allow the following driver time to respond should you need to slow down.

By holding back and maintaining a safe distance you will also have a better view of the road ahead, especially when following a larger vehicle. This is particularly important if you are considering overtaking, as you will have room to move out to improve your view and then accelerate past the other vehicle.

Act properly at road junctions

Act properly at road junctions with regard to: speed on approach; observation; approaching traffic; position before turning left and right; right corner cutting. On the approach adjust your *speed* so as to arrive at the hazard at a safe speed, allowing yourself plenty of time to make decisions about fina positioning and whether to stop or proceed. It is normally better to approach slightly too slowly rather than be rushed at the last minute, as this can cause unnecessary stops.

Your *observations* should include checking all round for different types of road user. For example, motorcyclists and cyclists are less easy to see and may be travelling faster than you think. Pedestrians often want to cross the road near to road junctions and they sometimes have difficulty in judging the speed and location of traffic approaching from different directions.

When you are emerging there is sometimes a need to stop and then creep forward to improve your view. Use any clues where possible – reflections in shop windows, looking through and under other vehicles, holding back slightly so that your view is not obstructed by other vehicles at the junction.

Approaching traffic

When turning right off a main road, make sure that you allow adequate time for any approaching traffic to pass before making your turn. However, if you have adjusted your speed correctly and have maintained effective observations, you may be able to time your turn effectively without the need to stop. When emerging into a main road make sure that you allow for the speed of the traffic travelling along the main road so that you do not impede them as you move away and build up your speed.

Positioning

Your position on the approach should depend on the type of junction and which direction you are taking. Look and plan well ahead, taking into account any road markings. Generally keep about one metre from the kerb (or in the centre of your lane) on the approach to a left turn and towards the centre of the road when turning right. Take up your position early – this will allow others to respond and to make their decisions in relation to what you are doing.

Right corner cutting

Cutting corners should be avoided – especially if your view into the other road is restricted. It is important that you should avoid having to change course or take evasive action part way round the corner.

Deal with other vehicles safely when overtaking, meeting, or crossing their path

Before overtaking you need to make sure that you can get past the other vehicle and return to your own side of the road without causing problems to either the oncoming traffic or the vehicle you are overtaking. Keep well back so that you obtain a good view of the road ahead and then make your move promptly and decisively when appropriate. If there is any doubt about the manoeuvre, don't overtake. When passing cyclists allow for sudden, unexpected changes of direction.

When turning at junctions, take into account the speed and movements of oncoming or approaching traffic, including motorcyclists and cyclists who are often travelling faster than you might appreciate. You should be able to complete your turn without causing other road users to slow down for you.

Position the vehicle correctly during normal driving; exercise lane discipline

Keep well to the left in normal driving, but don't weave in and out too much when passing parked obstructions. Avoid driving too close to the kerb in busy pedestrian areas. In one-way streets be guided by road markings and take up the correct road position as early as possible.

Lane markings should always be followed, as they are designed for effective use of road space and for efficient traffic flow. Avoid straddling two lanes or changing lanes unnecessarily or hurriedly at the last moment. Your examiner should give you directions early enough for you to respond, but if you do find yourself in the wrong lane avoid cutting across other vehicles. Your examiner will give you more directions to get you back onto the original route.

Allow adequate clearance to stationary vehicles and obstructions

Adequate clearance means allowing for doors opening, pedestrians stepping out from between cars and for the possibility of stationary vehicles suddenly moving off.

To allow adequate clearance you need to be at least a door's width away from the vehicle you are passing. If this is not possible, you should reduce your speed to an absolute minimum, especially if there is oncoming traffic. In congested areas drive a little further away from the kerb than normal if there are pedestrians about.

If there is an obstruction on your side of the road, you would normally expect to give way to any oncoming traffic, but don't automatically assume that other drivers will do the same when the obstruction is on their side. Allow plenty of room when passing the obstruction to allow for the unexpected, for example pedestrians moving off the pavement to avoid the obstruction.

Take appropriate action at pedestrian crossings

Your *speed* on the approach to *any pedestrian crossing* should be appropriate to:

● the type of crossing,
● the traffic conditions; and
● pedestrian activity.

You need to be able to stop in good time if necessary and without confusing or harassing any pedestrians who may be waiting to cross. Do not overtake on the approach.

At *zebra crossings* you should stop and give way to waiting pedestrians if it is safe for you to do so. Look and plan ahead, and make your intentions clear to the pedestrians. Use an arm signal if appropriate, but don't beckon them to cross. This signal could also be of benefit to an oncoming driver. Remember, you can never be certain of what the other driver might decide to do.

With light-controlled crossings, such as *pelicans*, *toucans* and *puffins*, be aware of pedestrians who are approaching and prepare for the lights to change. If there is a central refuge, treat the crossing as one complete crossing unless the two sides are staggered. The flashing amber light means that you should give way to any pedestrians on the crossing, but if there is no one using it you may proceed. However, you should keep an eye open for any pedestrians who do not necessarily obey the rules and who may start to cross.

At crossings controlled by *police*, *traffic wardens* or *school crossing wardens* you should wait if pedestrians are still crossing even if you have been given the signal to move away.

Keep checking all around for traffic and for pedestrians who may be crossing the road diagonally.

Consider using an arm signal to show that you are slowing or stopping. This can be an effective way of letting the pedestrian know that you are going to give way to them and allow them to make their own decision about crossing.

Select a safe position for normal stops

During your test, you will be asked on several occasions to find suitable places to stop. This is so that the examiner can assess not only *how* you stop and re-start, but also *where* you stop. Always ask yourself – 'Is it safe?', 'Is it legal?', 'Is it convenient?'

Make sure that you:

● obey any parking restrictions;

- avoid blocking any entrances or driveways; and
- are not too close to a road junction.

Allow yourself and other people room to move out.

Use the appropriate signals for stopping and for moving away if you feel they would help anyone. This includes any approaching drivers or cyclists; or pedestrians who may be crossing the road.

Show awareness and anticipation of the actions of pedestrians, cyclists, drivers

You can only *anticipate* if you constantly scan the road well ahead and make effective use of the available information. It is important that you anticipate not only what *is* happening and what *will* happen; but also what you can reasonably expect *might* happen. Maintain a constant check on and keep rechecking what is happening to the front and behind you on the road. By doing this, you can often turn the unexpected into the expected. Remember, what you *can't* see is even more important than what you *can* see because what you can't see *YOU DON'T KNOW*!

Keep scanning all around all the time so that you can take in the 'big picture'. Training yourself to spot and nominate hazards and potential hazards is an effective exercise. This does not need to involve giving a full running commentary, but simply itemising each problem area with a word or two as different situations arise.

Use of ancillary controls

This section covers your use of the minor controls as appropriate for different situations. It includes: the wipers and washers, side- and headlights, hazard warning lights, rear fog lights, and horn.

Hazard warning lights should normally only be used when the car is stationary. However, it is sometimes useful (and legal) to use them if you have to slow down rapidly on a fast, open road such as a dual carriageway or motorway. This should occur only if you feel that there is an immediate need to warn following traffic and should be a rare occurrence if you are looking and planning well ahead and keeping a safe distance.

Flashing headlamps should only be used to indicate your presence rather than as a particular signal. Their use can be particularly helpful on fast, open roads where the horn would be ineffective. If you respond to another driver's flashing lights, make sure that you are responding to what they are doing rather than to the signal itself and, before taking any action to proceed, make sure for yourself that the all-round situation is safe.

Rear fog lamps should be used in conditions of severely reduced visibility. Make sure the lights are switched off when they are no longer needed – they can mask the brake lights!

The *horn* should be used as an effective way of indicating your presence to other road users, especially where your view is restricted. If you think a pedestrian may not be aware of your presence, use it gently.

Avoid being (or even *appearing* to be) aggressive, as this can be distracting for other drivers and cause unnecessary conflict.

The marking system

The examiner will mark your driving faults on the test report form ADI25. The system of marking is very similar to that for the L test, except that the assessment of faults is to a higher standard.

A relatively minor error is regarded as a driving fault, and is marked with an oblique stroke '/'. This type of error might be marked if you make a mistake in your driving technique, or if you react inappropriately to a traffic situation.

A serious or potentially dangerous fault is marked as a single 'X'. These are usually faults involving situations where other road users might be put at risk or where you display a particular pattern of weakness in some aspect of your driving technique.

A fault that involves actual danger would be marked with a capital 'D'. This type of fault is when there is actual danger to yourself, your passengers or other road users.

If you have a maximum of six driving faults and no serious or dangerous faults, you will pass. With seven or more driving faults or with *any* single serious or dangerous fault you will fail.

The result is given to you at the end of the test.

For more detailed information on the examiner's marking system you should refer to the DSA publication *The Official DSA Guide for Driving Instructors*.

You must remember that there is no substitute for thorough and effective practical training from an experienced trainer.

The standard of driving needed to pass the Part 2 test is extremely high. Although you may have had several years of accident-free driving, you will almost certainly have developed a few habits that detract from the overall efficiency of your performance.

You will find it worthwhile to have an assessment with an experienced trainer early on in your course. This will give you more time to make any adjustments to the style of your driving so that the new style becomes your 'driving norm' well before you take the test.

In your general driving as well as in preparation for this test, always try to drive:

● smoothly;

● briskly;

● efficiently;

● economically;

● courteously; and

● with the vehicle under full control at all times.

Good forward planning and anticipation are the foundations of safe driving in today's traffic conditions. However, as an instructor you will need to be looking and planning even further ahead and working out all of the possibilities. This is essential when teaching inexperienced drivers how to anticipate and how to respond early enough to avoid potential problems.

Take the advice of your trainer or assessor. A failed test can mean a lost fee as well as the probable loss of confidence and a build of stress because of the limit on the number of attempts you can have.

Only take this test when you feel that your vehicle handling and road procedures are completely natural in all situations.

Good Luck!

7

The ADI Part 3 exam

THE TEST OF INSTRUCTIONAL ABILITY

This part of the ADI exam is designed to test your practical teaching skills and is structured in a way that will assess your ability to teach drivers at different levels of driving skill.

This is done by braking down the test into two phases. The first phase tests your ability to teach a novice or intermediate learner and the second assesses how you would deal with a more experienced learner.

The test is also designed to assess:

- the knowledge you gained while studying for the theory test; and
- whether you can put that knowledge into practice by teaching 'safe driving for life'.

The practical teaching skills described in this book will not only give you a good foundation on which to build your instructional ability and prepare you for this test, but should also provide you with an insight into what is involved in the ADI's everyday work.

Your trainer should teach you how to put your knowledge into practice in the car through:

- explanation;
- demonstration;

- role play; and
- practice.

THE SYLLABUS

The following is a list of the subjects you could be tested on. They are arranged under the two phases incorporated into the DSA marking forms (ADI 26/PT):

Phase 1 – Beginner	Phase 2 – Trained
1. Controls	Crossroads
2. Moving off/stopping, use of mirrors	Meet, cross and overtake other traffic, allowing clearance for other road-users and anticipation

Phase 1 – Partly Trained

3. Turn in the road	Approaching junctions to turn right or left
4. Reversing (either right or left)	Emerging
5. Emergency stop/use of mirrors (two separate subjects)	Progress/hesitancy and general road positioning
6. Pedestrian crossings/use of signals (two separate subjects)	Reverse parking
7. Approaching junctions to turn right or left	Pedestrian crossings/use of signals
8. T junctions – emerging	Meet, cross and overtake other traffic, allowing adequate clearance for other road-users and anticipation
9. Crossroads	Pedestrian crossings/use of signals
10. Meet, cross and overtake other traffic, allowing adequate clearance for other road-users and anticipation	Progress/hesitancy and general road positioning

PREPARING FOR THE PART 3 AND ALSO FOR YOUR EVERYDAY WORK AS AN ADI

When you take this test you will be tested on only two of the foregoing subjects, one from each phase. However, if your pupils are to be properly prepared for a lifetime's safe driving, a good training course should include not only these topics. You should also be given some tuition in those subjects listed in the DSA's *recommended syllabus for learners*, which you will find in their publication: *The Official Driving Test*.

Some of the other topics on which you should receive training are:

● Dual carriageways

● Roundabouts

● Rural roads and other driving situations

RESOURCE MATERIAL

As already explained, this part of the ADI exam is structured to test, through your instructional ability, your knowledge of the rules, regulations and procedures for safe driving. You will therefore need to refer to the same resource materials as listed in Chapter 5, 'The ADI theory test'.

PRESENTING THE LESSON

You will see from the foregoing *pre-set* test list that some of the subjects are included in both phases. This is designed to test your ability to adapt your tuition to suit the 'pupil's' needs. It is extremely important for you to understand the different practical teaching skills being assessed in each phase of the test. In simple terms they are as follows:

Phase 1 – structured to test your teaching skills. The 'pupil' being portrayed will be either a novice with no knowledge of the stated subject; or an intermediate learner with some prior knowledge.

Phase 2 – structured to test your assessment of the knowledge and skills of a more experienced pupil. It is also designed to test your ability to give further guidance and practice of the correct routines whilst at the same time ensuring that safe attitudes are encouraged.

Lesson notes

Part of your job as an instructor is to instil confidence in your pupils. To do this, you will need to display confidence in yourself. You will hardly do this if you have to open a textbook to give an explanation.

During the initial stages of your training you should have prepared some lesson notes listing the key elements of each subject in the syllabus. If you get sufficient training and practice before you take the Part 3, you should find that by this stage you no longer need them.

For in-car use, you may find *visual aids* more helpful. While your pupil can *see what you mean*, you can use them as a memory jogger. Using a picture, you can talk yourself through the elements of the subject as if you were carrying out the procedures as a driver.

Many candidates think visual aids should not be used on this test. However, you are supposed to be demonstrating what you would do as an instructor. If you think your 'pupil' is experiencing some difficulty in understanding a complicated procedure and would benefit from seeing a picture, use one!

Route Selection

Route planning is dealt with in detail in Chapter 4. However, don't worry about having to work out a route for your test in what may be an unfamiliar area to you.

For the purpose of this test your examiner will select the training route. This is because:

- You may not be familiar with the area.
- The examiner will know where to go to practise each specific subject.

At the beginning of the test your examiner will establish a method of communicating to you where you are required to take the 'pupil'.

Again, time constraints may mean that the route may not be one hundred per cent suitable. Don't let this be a distraction. Your examiner is also under the same constraints and has to adapt to the time available. You have to be prepared to adapt your instruction to suit where you are.

For example, if you were teaching a real novice how to move off and then stop, you would drive them to a quiet area with a long straight stretch of road away from other traffic and hazards. However, most test centres are situated in towns and you will not have the luxury of 10–15 minutes to drive away and find somewhere more appropriate. You will therefore need to adapt your tuition and time your instructions to get the 'pupil' moving away safely into gaps in the traffic. As long as you give the correct instructions, the 'pupil' should respond by carrying them out properly.

Adapting the lesson to the time available

- *Lesson planning* is dealt with in detail in Chapter 4 of this book. However, because of the time constraints, you need to adapt each lesson to fit the time available, while also ensuring that it suits the 'level of ability' of the 'pupil'. For example, if you were giving a normal on-road lesson of an hour's duration to a complete novice, you should have sufficient time to get them on the move by the end of it. However, since you will have less than half this time on the Part 3, you may not be able to achieve these same objectives.

You should bear in mind, however, that this is a practical test. Do not spend too much time stationary – but cover the necessary teaching points and get on the move so that your 'pupil' can *learn through practice*.

Each lesson should be planned as follows:

- Introductions. At this point you might find it helpful to jot down the 'pupil's' name and also the subject to be dealt with.
- Set the baseline by establishing prior knowledge.
- Explain any new elements for the 'beginner/novice'; or confirm prior knowledge of the more experienced 'pupil' through Q&A.
- Create opportunities for learning to take place through practice.
- Make corrections on the move as appropriate.
- Park up to discuss more serious problems.
- Create opportunities for correct procedures to be practised.
- Give positive feedback of progress, confirming areas that need more practice.

Setting the baseline for the lesson

No matter what subject is being taught and which phase you are dealing with, you will need to *set the baseline* for each lesson. To do this you need to establish what the 'pupil' already knows and can do by:

- listening carefully to the 'pupil's' description, making a mental note of previous experience;
- asking one or two questions to confirm knowledge of the subject;
- listening carefully to the responses for any hint of misunderstanding;
- correcting or confirming any response.

This procedure should take no longer than a couple of minutes – do not put the 'pupil' under any undue pressure by 'giving them a grilling'. Watch for, and respond to, body language and 'back off' if necessary.

Setting the objectives for the lesson

Any training session, no matter what the skill or subject being taught, should begin with a *statement of objectives*. All this needs to be is a simple statement such as: *'By the end of today's lesson you should understand and be able to deal with basic roundabouts.'*

Giving a briefing or explanation

We have already spoken about the time constraints of this test. Again, your explanation of the subject will have to be adapted to suit the time available – and of course it should also be adapted to suit any previous knowledge or experience your 'pupil' may have.

A few carefully worded questions at the beginning of each phase to establish the pupil's prior knowledge and understanding of the subject matter can prevent problems during the practical element of the test.

The questions will need to be:

- relevant to the pupil's perceived experience and
- to the subject matter.

As with setting the baseline for the lesson, ***listen carefully*** to the responses. It is your job to work out what the 'pupil' already knows, and your explanation should be designed to give any new information on the key elements of the subject, or to *top up* existing knowledge.

Please remember: *this is supposed to be a test of instructional ability.*

You are not expected to try to include in your briefings every single element you can think of relating to the subject matter.
YOU DO NOT HAVE THE TIME FOR THIS!

THINGS TO DO ON YOUR PART 3

A full breakdown of the subjects covered by the pre-set tests can be found in:

- *The Driving Instructors' Handbook*, and
- *The Official DSA Guide for Driving Instructors*.

However, our intention here is to list some of the most important things a good ADI should do. Remember for any learning to be effective, you have to ensure that you do not overload the 'pupil'. This means prioritising between what the 'pupil':

- *must know*;
- *should know*;
- *could know*.

This book is designed to help develop or improve your PTS. The content of each lesson (or pre-set test) is given in depth in *The Driving Instructor's Handbook* and *The DSA Official Guide for Driving Instructors*.

We are focusing here on the practical application of the routines in order to help you improve your 'pupils' skills. How much you include in your explanation at the beginning of a lesson will depend on:

- whether the 'pupil' is at the *Phase 1* or *Phase 2* stage of driving.

Or if it is at the *Phase 1* level:

- how much your 'pupil' already knows and understands about the subject.

Explanation of the controls (Pre-set Test 1)

At the test centre:

- Point out to your 'pupil' the importance of checking safety before getting in the car.
- Unless you are asked to deliver this lesson at the test centre, make use of the time driving to the training area to:
  - get to know the 'pupil' and find out why they want to learn;
  - establish validity of their licence and check eyesight requirements are met;
  - find out why they want to learn;
  - ask why they chose you; and
  - use the time to give talk through of what you are doing and why.

When you get to the training area:

- confirm the safety of opening doors and of getting out of passenger seat and into the driving seat;

- explain the importance of:
    - ensuring doors are closed properly;
    - correct seat adjustment – including head restraint and steering column, where appropriate;
    - correct mirror adjustment;
    - the use of seat belts and driver responsibility.

Dealing with the main controls

Your explanation of these should be organised in a way that avoids going backwards and forwards between hand and foot controls, thus make the learning more effective. Split your explanation into the main groups of:

- hand controls;
- foot controls;
- ancillary controls.

Allow plenty of 'hands on' stationary practice to confirm your terminology and to build up the 'pupil's' confidence. Include only those ancillary controls that are needed (*must know*).

Watch carefully for errors throughout. The following are just a few examples:

- door not properly closed;
- seat/back rake not adjusted properly;
- twists in the seatbelt;
- fingermarks on mirrors;
- mirrors not adjusted correctly;
- fidgeting with keys;
- hands taken off wheel to operate indicators;
- unsympathetic use of gear lever/handbrake/gas/clutch;
- wrong feet on pedals.

Many candidates perceive this test to be one of the easiest because it is carried out while stationary. However, many of the faults simulated by the examiner are introduced to test whether you are:

- listening carefully to the 'pupil's' questions and/or responses;
- giving clear instructions;
- watching closely for errors;

- able to give positive advice and correction;
- able to ensure that learning takes place.

Moving off and stopping (Pre-Set Test 2)

During the drive to the training area, use Q&A to establish prior knowledge.
  At the training area:

- Watch carefully, ensuring that the 'pupil' gets out of passenger seat and into driving seat safely;
- Encourage the 'pupil' to carry out 'cockpit drill' in correct sequence, watching for any errors that may hint at some misunderstanding;
- State the lesson objectives, ie to learn how to move off and stop safely.

During the lesson ensure that you include practical instruction, *and an explan ation of why*, on:

- mirrors and their use, including blind areas;
- the M–S–M routine;
- a little stationary practice in coordinating the foot controls;
- plenty of practice coordinating all of the controls for moving off and stopping;
- practice at moving off in different circumstances according to the opportunities that arise – for example, on the level up- and downhill;
- practical instruction in changing up and down gears;
- confirmation of safe and legal places for stopping.

Watch for 'pupil' errors such as:

- blind areas not being checked properly – it is far more effective to ask: 'Is there anyone in the blind area?' than giving an instruction to: 'Have a quick look around.'
- incorrect coordination of gas and clutch – by being *totally in tune with your car* and giving positive correction in good time, you should be able to prevent misuse of the controls, stalls and other problems. Remember, you are supposed to be building up your 'pupil's' confidence;
- looking down at the controls when the eyes should be focused on looking ahead;

- wandering off course by looking at the kerb, watching other cars as they overtake, or trying to use the centre line as a guide;
- stopping in unsafe places.

During the lesson give positive advice to develop car control skills. Also introduce an element of hazard perception and defensive driving by making the 'pupil' aware of the need to respond to other road users.

Turn in the road/left and right reversing and reverse parking (Pre-Set Tests 3/4/6)

The lesson structure for teaching all of the manoeuvre exercises is very similar. After you have established whether or not the 'pupil' has any previous experience, you need to confirm their knowledge and understanding of:

- coordination of all of the controls;
- effective observations throughout – explain about priorities and how to respond to others;
- accuracy – reasonable accuracy should be aimed at, not perfection.

Because of the time limit, there is not normally sufficient time to give an explanation and a separate demonstration. However, if you think a demonstration would be beneficial, consider combining the two and talk yourself through the exercise while the 'pupil' watches and listens. *If you go for this option, your demonstration should be a good one!*

During the lesson watch for, and try to avoid through positive correction, errors such as the 'pupil's':

- poor coordination of the foot controls. This could be caused by (a) a lack of understanding and insufficient practice at balancing the clutch – confirm by asking whether the 'pupil' knows how to do this, and get them to explain how they would creep forwards to get a better view at a blind junction – or (b) something as basic as not adjusting the seat properly – check on this by ensuring that the 'cockpit drill' is carried out correctly;
- not checking all around for others or not responding properly to them – if you see another road user approaching, get the 'pupil' to pause, encourage them to have a good look around and then wait until it's safe to proceed;
- not looking in the direction the wheel is being turned or where they want the car to go.

Try to ensure, through positive instruction, correction and practice, that a degree of success is achieved.

Emergency stop and use of mirrors (Pre-Set Test 5)

Use of mirrors

Use the first part of the lesson to confirm the 'pupil's' knowledge of:

- mirror adjustment;
- blind areas;
- M–S–M routine for moving off, changing speed and direction, stopping;
- how to respond safely to what is happening behind.

Use the initial drive to check for:

- ineffective checks of the blind areas;
- exaggerated head movement – make sure that the mirrors are properly adjusted;
- out-of sequence application of the M–S–M routine;
- incorrect response to what is happening behind;
- lack of use of door mirrors before changing position.

Before explaining about stopping in emergency situations, give some positive feedback and corrective advice on any weaknesses. Confirm the need for good drivers to remain fully aware of what is happening all around them all of the time.

Emergency stop

Confirm the need for looking and planning well ahead and of anticipating what might happen (hazard perception). Give practical advice and examples on where the need to stop quickly may arise. Explain how to:

- react promptly;
- use the footbrake and clutch;
- maintain steering control;
- avoid skidding;
- correct skids;
- check all around before driving away.

Before moving away, make sure you demonstrate the signal you will be using when you want the 'pupil' to stop.

By the end of the session, you should be able to get the 'pupil' to carry out safely all of the foregoing items. During practice, watch for:

● slow reactions and movements between the gas and brake pedals;

● harsh or too gentle use of the brake;

● the left hand being taken off the wheel before the car has stopped;

● the clutch being pushed down too early/too late;

● lack of precautions before starting up the engine after a stall;

● lack of effective observations, particularly over the left shoulder, before moving off again.

Pedestrian crossings and the use of signals (Pre-Set Tests 6/7/9)

Following the usual pattern of lesson planning, find out what the 'pupil' already knows. Also bear in mind that all of your 'pupils' will have used pedestrian crossings whether on foot or behind the wheel.

With an intermediate learner, build on this knowledge to confirm the correct procedures for dealing with the different types of crossing. (Refer to *The Driving Instructor's Handbook* and *The Official DSA Guide for Driving Instructors*.) Remember this is a practical test. Keep your explanation to the key points in order to allow plenty of time for practice.

If you are dealing with a more experienced 'pupil' (Phase 2), use Q&A to establish any problem areas and get on the move so that you can make an initial assessment. You should then create opportunities for applying any remedial advice.

Before driving away confirm the 'pupil's' knowledge of using the different methods of signalling to warn or inform other road users of their presence or intentions. Allow for a demonstration of the arm signal for stopping, confirming why this could be beneficial at pedestrian crossings if the conditions or situation call for it.

The following is a list of some of the aspects that during the drive you should be watching for and offering practical advice on.

Indicators/flashing lights/arm signals/horn

● putting on the correct signal – relate the indicator going in the same direction in which the wheel is to be turned;

- cancelling signals after use or when the self-cancelling device doesn't work;
- applying any signals that cancel prematurely;
- ensuring that any signals for stopping are cancelled before moving off;
- deciding when signals are needed and discriminating against those not required;
- checking the mirrors before deciding on the need and timing of signals;
- using the horn when it would be beneficial to someone;
- responding safely to other drivers' signals.

Watch out for any incorrect response to the signals of others and for unsafe signals being given, for example beckoning others to proceed.

Pedestrian crossings

Whether you are talking an 'intermediate learner' through, or are assessing a more advanced 'pupil', you should ensure that the correct routines are applied on the approach to all types of crossing. Make sure your 'pupil':

- looks and plans well ahead;
- is anticipating, and responding to, what *could* happen as well as what is happening;
- demonstrates their understanding of the rules by:
  - applying the correct hazard routine, ie M–S–M;
  - approaching at a speed that will allow safe stopping when necessary;
  - giving signals when appropriate;
  - securing the car properly;
  - moving away safely.

Turning left and right and emerging at junctions and crossroads (Pre-Set Tests 1/3/4/7/8/9)

As with other topics, you first of all need to establish the baseline for the lesson so that it will be pitched at the correct level for the 'pupil'.

Find out by asking a few questions, what the 'pupil' knows about the routine for approaching junctions and emerging at junctions. For example:

Phase 1

- Have you turned left or right at junctions before?

- Tell me what routine you will be applying.
- Where should you look before you turn?
- Have you dealt with crossroads before?
- What extra observations will you need to make?
- Who has priority at an uncontrolled crossroads?
- What is the sequence of traffic lights?

Phase 2

- Do you understand why you failed your test for emerging?
- Can you remember the circumstances?
- Why is it important to keep looking both ways at junctions?
- What should you look for before turning into a side road?
- What does a green traffic light mean?

Whatever the level of your 'pupil', you should ensure that the correct routines are applied. Where there are weaknesses or misunderstandings you must create opportunities to practice so that positive learning or improvement takes place.

For all types of junction ensure that:

- the M–S–M routine is applied in the correct sequence;
- signals are timed properly;
- full control of the car is maintained through correct use of the brakes and gears;
- positioning is appropriate for the direction, the width of the road and the presence of other road users;
- full all-round observations are made – keep checking where your 'pupil' is looking as well as that it will be safe for them to emerge; for example, if your 'pupil' is not looking effectively in all directions, you can encourage this by saying something like:
    - 'Keep looking both ways.'
    - 'How far can you see?'
    - 'Can you see past that wall?'
    - 'Are you checking in all directions?'

Only allow your 'pupil' to emerge when it is safe to do so.

No matter what the level of ability of your 'pupil', you are responsible for their safety, the safety of other road users and, of course, of yourself. Don't let an unsafe situation arise that could put someone at risk when it could easily be avoided with a simple command, such as 'Wait'. (Fault analysis is dealt with in detail in Chapter 4.)

Meet, cross, overtake other traffic, allowing adequate clearance for other road users and anticipation (Pre-Set Tests 2/8/10)

You will normally only be asked to deal with three of these five topics. It is particularly vital to listen extremely carefully and to jot down on your pad those topics you are to work on. This should help avoid you teaching the 'pupil' to overtake when you have been asked to deal with meeting other traffic and allowing adequate clearances.

As with teaching junctions, whatever the level of knowledge and ability of your 'pupil', you should ensure that the correct routines are applied. These topics create the ideal opportunity to develop your 'pupil's' hazard perception skills.

Where there are weaknesses or misunderstandings you must create opportunities to practise so that positive learning or improvement takes place and safe attitudes are developed. In all circumstances, you must ensure that the correct procedures are applied.

Meeting other traffic and allowing adequate clearances

- Approaching all hazards, the M–S–M routine should be seen to be applied.
- Priority is given to others when appropriate. This applies no matter on which side of the road an obstruction is on.
- Adequate clearances are given and the 'pupil' recognises what these are and why they are necessary.

Crossing other traffic and overtaking

- When turning right, ensure that the 'pupil' gives priority to oncoming traffic when appropriate.
- When approaching road junctions, ensure that the 'pupil' looks before turning into them.
- Encourage safe attitudes towards overtaking. Overtaking can often be a difficult subject as opportunities to teach it may not arise and are difficult to create. It is your responsibility, however, to encourage safe attitudes

towards this manoeuvre. Explain how to overtake, emphasising the ongoing importance of all-round observations throughout and the slight difference in the application of the M–S–M routine. (See *The Driving Instructor's Handbook*.)

Anticipation

Teaching anticipation is an ongoing process and should begin from lesson one. No matter what level of ability the 'pupil' has achieved, you should take all opportunities that arise to teach awareness, anticipation and hazard perception.

When you see a problem in the road ahead and your 'pupil' is not responding, you should do all you can to keep the environment safe.

If your 'pupil' has very little experience, you will need to talk them through.

If the 'pupil' is more advanced, you should give them the opportunity to avoid the problem by asking a thought-provoking question such as 'Whose priority is it ahead? Do you think you can get through the gap safely because I wouldn't be going through it?'

It is your job to ensure that some positive learning takes place, even when a mistake has occurred.

Progress, hesitancy and positioning (Pre-set Test 10)

To be an effective instructor you need to teach new drivers the importance of:

● being in the correct position on the road at all times; and of
● making safe progress to keep the traffic moving, without putting anyone at risk.

Positioning

Ensure that your pupil:

● maintains the correct position for driving along;
● positions correctly when turning left and right;
● adapts their position appropriately for the width of the road;
● drives in the centre of their lane when there is more than one lane in each direction;
● reads signs and markings and complies with them;
● makes any lane changes gradually and safely, applying the M–S–M;
● maintains lane discipline throughout roundabouts.

Progress/hesitancy

Ensure that your pupil:

- moves off promptly when safe;
- builds up speed and changes up through the gears positively;
- uses all of the gears as appropriate;
- drives up to the speed limit where safe to do so;
- uses all safe opportunities to proceed into gaps in the traffic at junctions.

Roundabouts and dual carriageways

Although these are not dealt with specifically as pre-set test subjects on the Part 3, you have a responsibility to teach new drivers how to deal with them. In any case, most test centres are situated in areas where there are these types of road layouts. Even if you don't have to give an explanation or 'briefing' on your test, you may have to give some talk-through tuition to your Phase 1 'learner'; or to ensure that your Phase 2 'pupil' is putting into practice safe routines.

Be prepared!

You must be prepared to teach 'Safe driving for life'.

No matter what subject you get or what the 'pupil's' standard is, you must ensure that, by the end of each 'lesson', SOME LEARNING HAS TAKEN PLACE.

ADAPTING TO THE ROLE-PLAY SITUATION

Role play is often used in the training environment to create situations where either learning or assessment of specific areas of skills can take place in safety.

In the case of the ADI exam, if a real learner were used, it would be extremely difficult to set up situations that would test these areas of your teaching and assessment ability.

While preparing for the Part 3, you should have become accustomed to your trainer role-playing different learners in a variety of situations. This should stand you in good stead for the test.

One of the most difficult drawbacks, however, is that you will know in your own mind that the person sitting beside you 'putting on an act as a learner' is really someone with a great deal of knowledge about driving.

You must try to overcome this barrier by being prepared to 'take part in the game'. Have the courage of your convictions that you have a good deal of knowledge – gained through studying for the test of theory – and that your driving skills have been proved by your passing the Part 2. All you have to do now is pass on that knowledge and ensure that the person beside you is advised on how these principles should be applied on the road.

To 'take part in the game' you must:

● concentrate;
● listen very carefully to the description of the 'pupil' being portrayed;
● either make a mental note, or write down anything you think is not understood;
● ask questions relevant to the subject;
● listen carefully to the responses; and
● be prepared to give extra information or corrective advice.

By the time you have done this, you should have started to relax a little and be settling into your role as the instructor. The following are a few sample questions.

General introduction questions.

● How long have you been learning?
● Are you able to practise between your lessons?

The answers given by your 'pupil' may generate other questions. If the 'pupil' is someone with very little experience and you have been asked to teach a manoeuvre, you could ask:

● Have you done any reversing yet?
● Can you move off on hills and from behind parked cars?

Following this you should be able to make a definite link to the lesson and ask the 'pupil' to:

● Tell me how you would control the car so as to creep forwards slowly to get a better view at a blind junction.

With a phase 2 'pupil', you could ask

- Have you taken a test yet?
- Can you remember what the examiner discussed with you at the end of it?

The roles used in the test

Examiners conducting the ADI exams have all been trained in playing different roles. The role selected will depend on the:

- subject being taught;
- level of ability of the 'pupil';
- aspect of your teaching skill that is being assessed.

Linked to the above, the examiner will either play a *proactive* or a *reactive* part and this will be done through one of the following roles:

- negative;
- simple;
- average;
- testing; and
- knowledgeable.

Normally the examiner will begin each phase in the *proactive* role in order to introduce realistic faults. This will then enable an assessment of whether or not you are responding by giving correct instruction to which the examiner will react positively.

Proactive

Should you give no positive advice, the examiner will remain in this role and continue making similar mistakes. Questions may then be asked in order to give you a prompt and to test your flexibility. If this happens, the examiner is asking you for more help and information. Don't ignore this hint – remember to teach safe driving, the 'learner' needs to have good reasons for doing things.

Roles played under this heading are:

- *Negative* – the SE will wait for you to use Q&A to establish knowledge and understanding and when you ask 'Did you understand that?' replies simply 'Yes'.

- *Simple* – does not respond to technical instruction, waiting for you to adjust the level of your terminology to suit the 'pupil'.

- *Average* – asks questions in a normal way and relevant to the subject.

- *Testing* – the 'pupil's' questions go beyond what is being taught. For example 'What if …? The examiner will then wait for you to deal positively with this.

- *Knowledgeable* – this is the 'know it all pupil' who will challenge everything you say and will pick up on any doubtful instruction by asking: 'Why must I do that then?'.

Reactive

Unless possible danger is involved, whether your instruction is correct, incorrect or late, the examiner will do exactly as told.

Roles played under this heading are:

- *Negative* – the SE will respond normally to your questions and may ask further questions to clarify a point.

- *Simple* – when you adjust the level of your instruction to suit the 'pupil', the SE queries you on more technical matters.

- *Average* – your instructions, whether correct or incorrect, will be followed to the letter, unless it is unsafe.

- *Testing* – when you react and take control, the SE will keep to the subject but will be ready for the 'What if …?'

- *Knowledgeable* – when you take control, the SE will offer less challenges but will pick up on any incorrect instruction by saying, for example, 'But my last instructor said …'.

The SE will use a role felt to be appropriate for the 'pupil' and level of ability being portrayed. They do not normally play the same type of personality for both phases of the test and rarely choose to play the *average* learner.

Whatever two roles your examiner plays, you must try to become positively involved and deal with each in a way that is:

- sensitive to their needs;

- tactful – you do not want to insult your 'pupil';

- adjusted to suit any lack of response;

- likely to result in positive learning taking place.

THE MARKING SYSTEM

Although the information is readily available to trainee instructors, the PST26 marking sheets are primarily for the examiners' use. You should refer to these to familiarise yourself with the driving topics and their component elements that you will have to teach new drivers.

Many candidates in the Part 3 believe that they have to include in their 'briefings' all of the elements listed on the left-hand side of the forms. However, if you do this for each 'pupil' and in each phase, you may end up spending too much time stationary when you should be either teaching or correcting practically.

At the end of each phase, an assessment will be made and you must try to ensure during your test that:

- each 'pupil' learns about, and how to do, something;
- understanding is achieved;
- some improvement of existing skills takes place;
- a change in attitude is achieved;
- your instruction is positive;
- no potentially dangerous situations are allowed to develop;
- each 'pupil' is dealt with tactfully;
- the instruction is pitched at the correct level;
- most of the faults are identified and analysed;
- positive feedback and remedial advice is given and
- opportunities are taken to practice correct procedures.

Your instruction will be assessed under the following headings:

1. *Core competencies*
   - identification of faults;
   - fault analysis;
   - remedial action.

2. *Instructional techniques*
   - level of instruction;
   - planning;
   - control of lesson;
   - communication;

- Q&A techniques;
- feedback/encouragement.
- use of controls.

3. *Instructor characteristics*
   - attitude and approach to 'pupil'.

For a detailed analysis of how the Part 3 is marked, refer to *The Driving Instructor's Handbook* and *The Official DSA Guide for Driving Instructors*. You will also find more information on fault assessment in Chapter 4 of this book.

ON THE DAY OF THE TEST

If you have sufficient training and have prepared your lesson plans and visual aids properly, you should feel confident that you can deal positively with the two pupils being portrayed.

Remember to take the relevant documents with you and plan on arriving at the test centre a few minutes early. Also remember that, because of the volume of traffic and other possible hold-ups, journey times are extremely difficult to plan precisely. If you have to rush to get there, you are not going to be in the right frame of mind for a test!

As well as making sure your car is roadworthy and clean (see *The ADI 14*), some of the 'extras' you might take with you include:

- a round tray for steering practice;
- a window leather;
- sunglasses;
- some mints – to combat the 'dry mouth' feeling;
- a soft drink.

SOME COMMON REASONS FOR FAILING THE PART 3

There is a high failure rate for this part of the ADI exam. Here are some of the reasons:

- lack of good training and poor preparation;

- inability to adapt to the role-play situation and to treat the examiner as a learner;
- failure to listen properly to the description and level of ability of the 'pupil';
- inadequate or incorrect use of Q&A and failing to listen to answers;
- an inadequate briefing or introduction to the lesson;
- inadequate knowledge of the subject, resulting in a poor explanation and practical session;
- spending too much time on the briefing, leaving inadequate time for effective learning to take place;
- under-instruction, resulting from expecting too much from the 'learner' and not giving enough help for them to improve;
- over-instruction, resulting from giving too much information and not responding to the 'pupil's' obvious driving ability;
- lack of control of the lesson by allowing unsympathetic use of the car or unsafe actions on the road with the Phase 1 'pupil', and not taking opportunities to stop and discuss major problems with the Phase 2 'pupil'. This sometimes leads to a 'takeover' by the 'pupil' and more and more errors being introduced and going uncorrected;
- failure to correct minor problems on the move;
- poor fault assessment and inadequate analysis, leading to failure to give remedial advice or allow practice to improve.
- failure to use effective Q&A or lack of response to feedback given;
- failure to offer positive praise and encouragement.

If:

- you stay cool, calm and collected and are firm, fair and friendly;
- you apply all of the PTS covered in this book;
- your instruction is all positive; and
- each of your 'pupils' learns something;

you should have no trouble in passing the test of instructional ability.

Good luck!

8

The ADI Check Test

Changes to the ADI regime over the past few years mean that the Check Test is assessed to the same criteria as the Part 3 Test of Instructional Ability. This means that qualified instructors have to meet the same rigorous standards as new instructors. This is to ensure that, irrespective of how long ADIs have been registered, the standard of instruction given to all fee-paying customers is of a reasonable and consistent standard.

Because of the higher standards now required for instructors to achieve the minimum acceptable grade of 4, many are worried about their Check Test, particularly in view of the fact that more ADIs are being removed from the Register for substandard tuition than ever before. Sometimes, especially if it is an instructor's first Check Test after qualifying, it is 'fear of the unknown' that causes the problem.

This unfounded fear often results in instructors presenting lessons differently from their normal pattern, simply because they are being 'watched'.

All instructors should welcome the Check Test as an opportunity to demonstrate their teaching ability and to benefit from the advice offered by their Supervising Examiner.

There is a saying that:

POOR PREPARATION = POOR PRESENTATION

This chapter offers advice to all instructors, no matter what their experience, on how to properly prepare for the Check Test.

Good application of the practical teaching skills in this book, and an understanding of how your performance will be assessed against the set criteria, should give you greater confidence when you have your Check Test. It will also help ensure that you achieve the best possible grading for your ability.

Do not try to 'stage' what you think to be an easy lesson by presenting a very good learner dealing with an obviously well-rehearsed subject. Also try to avoid putting on a special show that is different from the way you normally teach. Because your pupil sees you behaving differently he or she may become confused. This confusion could well lead to them making more mistakes than normal and both of you becoming frustrated.

A pupil who is struggling with a subject may well present a better opportunity for you to display your true skills. It will also make it easier for you and the pupil to concentrate on the job in hand rather than worrying about the SE sitting in the back of the car.

Any test is of little value if the information and feedback gained is not then fed back into the learning process. This means if you do not give a true picture of your teaching skills, how can the SE judge them properly, how can an objective assessment be made and how can corrective advice be given?

The 'L' Test, the ADI practical entrance exam and the Check Test are all based on the following principle:

Failure to meet the criteria indicates that the performance is incomplete and needs modifying in some way.

It would be unreasonable to say to one of your pupils who failed the 'L' test, 'Well, you had your chance and you blew it!' Surely, what you would do is book further lessons for that pupil to bring about any improvement necessary, before retaking the test.

Irrespective of the grading you receive, you should be prepared to modify your instruction to take into account any weaknesses identified. On your next Check Test, the SE will be looking to see that any previous recommendations have been implemented.

Some driving instructors find it very difficult to stand back and look at what they are doing in the way that the examiner is able to. They cannot see the wood for the trees! They are often so involved in the teaching that they cannot see whether any learning is taking place.

The Check Test is useful to instructors in that it provides accessible information that can be used to improve the amount of learning taking place during driving lessons.

> *You should see the Check Test as being an independent assessment of your teaching ability, the cost of which is included in your registration fee.*

The test is designed so that the examiner can:

● ASSESS your teaching ability;
● ADVISE you of the outcome and the grading given; and
● ASSIST you to make improvements by giving you feedback.

It is natural to be nervous on the test. This, too, is part of your learning process as it will allow you to know first hand what your pupils feel like when they are taking the 'L' test. However, once your natural enthusiasm and the desire to get the best out of your pupil come into play, you should be able to forget the examiner and concentrate instead on giving a normal lesson.

In any examination or test, careful preparation will greatly improve the chances of success. The Check Test is no different.

You need to know:

● what the Check Test is, why it is in place and who conducts it;
● where Check Tests are carried out;
● how the test is conducted;
● how to prepare for your Check Test;
● how to present the lesson;
● how to get the best possible grading;
● the result.

To comply with the regulations, after qualifying as an ADI you have to undergo a Check Test whenever required to do so by the Registrar. The statutory requirement is simply an opportunity for the SE to check that your instruction is up to the level required for you to remain on the Register.

The testing and checking of driving instructors is the responsibility of a relatively small team of the DSA's Supervising Examiners who have undertaken extensive specialist training. You and your pupil should be aware that the Check Test is not related to the 'L' driver testing system. The examiner is there to assess the quality of the instruction being given and not your pupil's driving.

WHEN AND WHERE CHECK TESTS WILL BE CARRIED OUT

If you have recently qualified as an ADI, the SE for your area will soon contact you at your home address to invite you to attend for a Check Test. You will be given a date and time, and the test will start from either the SE's office or from your local driving test centre. If the SE's office is in an area which you are not familiar with, you can elect to take it instead from your local 'L' test centre. You should acknowledge the invitation as soon as possible, letting the SE know immediately if you are unable to attend or if you wish to change the venue.

The first Check Test is 'educational' in that it is designed to let your local SE, who may not be the one who tested you on the Part 3 exam, see your work and let you know if there is anything which needs improving.

Provided that your instruction was satisfactory, you will be given a grading, otherwise you will be invited to attend another Check Test within a few months.

If you have been qualified for some time, you will periodically be invited to attend for a Check Test. The grading you received on your last Check Test will determine how soon you will be required to undertake a further test.

Again, you should acknowledge the invitation as soon as possible, letting the SE know if you cannot keep the appointment or wish to change the venue. In this case another date and time, or venue, will be offered.

The Check Test will normally be conducted during the SE's normal working hours – ie, Mondays to Thursdays between 8.30 am and 5.00 pm. If you do not have a pupil available at that time, you may give instruction to a full licence holder, as long as this person is not an ADI. You are not allowed to use another ADI as a pupil. If you cannot arrange for a learner or full licence holder to accompany you for your Check Test, then rather than postpone the appointment, the SE may opt to 'role-play' the part of a learner.

HOW THE CHECK TEST IS CONDUCTED

The SE will accompany you while you are giving a driving lesson to a pupil. You are assessed in much the same way as in the ADI examinations but, because the driving lesson is longer than each phase of the Part 3, it allows more time for the pupil to practise driving. The SE will be looking for:

- the method, clarity, adequacy and correctness of your instruction;

- your observation and correction of the pupil's errors; and

- your manner, patience and tact in dealing with the pupil, and your ability to inspire confidence.

Remember that the SE is assessing your ability to instruct and not your pupil's ability to drive. You can give a lesson to a driver at any level of ability – a total novice, an 'experienced' learner or a full licence holder – but the lesson must be tailored to suit the needs of the pupil.

PREPARING FOR YOUR CHECK TEST

The vehicle in which you conduct your lesson should be safe and reliable, and must carry 'L' plates if you are teaching a pupil who has a provisional licence. If the lesson is conducted in your own or a school car, this should not be a problem. If the lesson is in the pupil's car, it would be sensible to check on the state of the vehicle and, of course, the insurance beforehand. Your ADI certificate must be displayed if you are charging a fee for the lesson.

How you prepare for the lesson should really be no different to what you do for any other lesson. However, you should also be ready to explain to the SE some background information about the pupil and about the lesson you intend to give.

In particular you should let the SE know:

- whether the person is a regular pupil of yours;

- what you know about the pupil's progress;

- what professional instruction the pupil has received;

- whether they are having any private practice;

- any strengths or weaknesses of which you are aware; and

- your lesson plan.

Any teaching aids that you normally use should be prepared in advance. They should be ready and available for use as and when required during the lesson.

Notes and any other written material should only be used for reference and should not be read word for word.

PRESENTING THE LESSON

The SE wants to see a 'normal' lesson. Do not try to put on a special show. Presenting a lesson is covered in full detail in Chapter 4, but before the lesson begins you need to take account of the following special requirements.

- Structure the lesson to last about an hour but you will have to allow additional time for discussion with the SE.
- Introduce the pupil to the SE and explain the purpose of the visit.
- Emphasise to the pupil that it is you who is being checked.
- Encourage the pupil to behave normally and to ask questions if there is anything that has not been understood.
- Remind the pupil that because of the extra weight in the back, the car may handle slightly differently.

At the beginning of the lesson, you may need to confirm with a short recap what was covered in the previous lesson. Asking a couple of questions should tell you whether the pupil has remembered the key points.

Explain to the pupil what is going to be covered in the lesson. This will also let the SE know what the objectives are.

Using your own style, adapt your method of instruction to suit the pupil's ability, personality and progress.

The SE will be assessing your fault identification, analysis and correction. Any remedial advice you give will be assessed for its effectiveness.

If the pupil is not someone whom teach regularly, make sure that you find out about any previous experience by asking appropriate questions and by inviting the pupil to ask questions.

Although you will have set objectives for the lesson, be prepared to vary your original plan if necessary. For example, if serious problems arise in other areas, concentrate on correcting these. Give the pupil your reasons for changing the lesson plan and explain that the original topic will be covered in a future lesson.

> *Your explanations should be methodical and systematic, with a clear definition of the key points of any new subject. Avoid excessive verbalisation or repetition and make sure that the information you give is correct. Encourage the pupil to ask questions if you think that any misunderstanding may have occurred. Your answers should be correct and in sufficient detail for the needs of the pupil.*

Avoid giving any complicated instructions on the move as this will only distract the pupil and may divert attention away from the driving task. If the pupil asks questions while driving along, answer only briefly, saying 'I want to talk about that when we stop'.

Route directions should be given clearly and in good time. Encourage your pupil to read the road signs and markings. How much guidance you give to the pupil will depend on ability and experience.

Two very common instructional errors arise from not matching the level of instruction to the ability of the pupil. These are: UNDER-INSTRUCTION and OVER-INSTRUCTION.

Under-instruction

This often happens when an instructor tries to conduct a mock test letting the pupil drive around and saying nothing until the end. This gives the SE very little information about the method of instruction. Even if the pupil is driving reasonably well, a few mistakes are bound to occur and the instructor should work on the positive correction of them.

Many experienced instructors feel that if positive correction is given to a pupil at test standard, it will be classed as 'prompting' or 'over-instruction'. However, positive learning is more likely to take place if you draw the pupil's attention to a problem before it gets too serious. Allowing a dangerous situation to develop and then discussing it later is negative or retrospective correction and is not good teaching practice.

For example, there may be an obstruction on the left and you don't feel that it would be safe to allow your pupil to drive through because of approaching traffic. The pupil, however, is making no attempt to slow down and is obviously heading for the gap. To instigate some positive action to give way, you could ask, 'Do you think that it is safe to go for that gap? – because I wouldn't want to try it'.

This 'prompting' would be far safer than allowing the pupil to scrape through the gap with unsafe margins for error, then saying, 'You shouldn't have gone through that gap – it was dangerous'.

Over-instruction

Unless the pupil is in the very early stages of instruction, or practising a new skill for the first time, try to avoid 'talking them round'. Over-instruction will deter the pupil from thinking and making decisions, which will inhibit progress.

Over-instruction often occurs when the pupil is practising new skills, mixed in with consolidating existing skills. For example, you may be teaching the turn in the road and giving a complete talk-through, but forget that the pupil already knows how to move off and stop. Try to restrict your talk-through to the aspects of the manoeuvre that are new to the pupil.

Use of the Question and Answer (Q&A) technique is covered in detail in Chapter 4. This method of teaching can help to encourage pupils to look and plan ahead. Poor Q&A is a common reason for failing the Check Test. It is vital, therefore, that you fully understand how to apply it effectively. Using good Q&A will:

- tell you what the pupil is thinking;
- test the pupil's knowledge and understanding;
- encourage the pupil to think more about solving problems and making decisions;
- ensure the pupil is participating in the lesson and in the learning process.

For example, if your pupil continually drives too close to parked vehicles, you could ask: 'What should you be looking for around these parked cars?' Or if bends are approached at too high a speed: 'What will you do if there is an obstruction around the bend?'

Because no two situations are the same, each drive should prompt different questions. Your skill in choosing the most appropriate one, while avoiding over-instruction, will depend on:

- the pupil's ability;
- what is happening in your vehicle;
- what is happening outside the vehicle;
- the presence and actions of other road users;
- the weather, road conditions and visibility;
- road signs and markings;
- the urgency of any required action.

Generally speaking, less experienced pupils are likely to need more questions. However, these should be relatively straightforward and simple. You will probably need to use less questions with the more experienced pupils. However, these should be more searching. Some instructors find it difficult to 'let go of the reins' and fire too many unnecessary questions. The SE may interpret this as *over-instruction*. Remember, the sooner pupils are allowed to make their own decisions, the quicker they will learn.

As an instructor, knowing when to shut up is as important as knowing when to speak!

The question and answer technique may be useful to encourage the pupil to look and plan ahead. It will also tell you what the pupil is thinking. Using the Q&A technique not only tests the pupil's knowledge and understanding, but encourages them to think more about solving problems and making their own decisions. This should also result in a greater degree of participation in the learning task and a better understanding of safe driving principles.

For example, if you are following a bus, its brake lights come on and you see passengers getting up, ask the question: 'What do you think the bus is going to do?', or, if you see the dustbins on the pavements, ask: 'What activity could you be expecting to see in this area today?'

Observation and proper correction of errors

Stay alert and try to show an interest in the pupil. Continually look for ways in which to improve their performance. You should recognise all faults and differentiate between those which require immediate attention and those that are only one-off minor errors.

Constant 'nit-picking' may undermine the confidence of the pupil. Where minor errors occur in isolation that do not affect safety or control, it may be better not to mention them. This applies particularly in the early stages when the pupil may be under pressure while learning new skills. It can, however, also apply in the later stages of learning. For example, while waiting at a red traffic light with the handbrake on and neutral selected, your pupil takes one hand off the wheel to rub an eye. As the car is secured and the discomfort could cause a distraction, is it really necessary for you to tell your pupil to keep both hands on the wheel?

The causes and consequences of errors should be identified, together with the actions required to prevent recurrence. It is important that corrections are made in a positive manner. For example, 'Drive in the centre of your lane' is much better than 'Don't drive on the white line'. The latter comment only confirms and reinforces what should *not* be done without indicating the correct position on the road.

> *It is no good explaining what the pupil did wrong if you do not explain WHY it is important.*

A good instructor will ask a pupil: 'Why do you think we should keep in the middle of our lane?'

You should identify and correct the *causes* of any errors and not just the effect of them. For example, if your pupil emerges from a junction without taking effective observation, it should tell you that the potential danger from oncoming traffic has not been understood. Rather than merely confirming the error by saying, 'You emerged before you could see properly', it is better to explain the importance of the creep and peep routine.

Whether or not the pupil has understood about limited zones of vision will subsequently be shown by their response in a similar situation. If they demonstrate an ability to use the creep and peep routine, your explanation has obviously been effective. If the pupil still emerges without taking effective observations, then the potential for danger has still not been understood and may be caused by another problem, such as an inability to judge speed. A more detailed explanation may be necessary, followed by further practice.

Because of the need for you to be constantly checking all around, it is not always possible to monitor every single mirror check. To avoid any arguments which might arise from undue criticism, rather than stating 'You didn't check your mirrors!', it may be better to ask 'Did you check the mirror before signalling?'

The response is not really important. What does matter is that the pupil will know whether or not the mirror was checked. Your question will therefore have had the desired effect of making the pupil think about using the mirrors. You can then expand on this by asking 'Why is it important to check the mirrors before signalling?'

Manner, patience, tact and the ability to inspire confidence

MANNER – You should try to create a professional but relaxed atmosphere in the car, without becoming over-familiar. How you address your pupils will depend on yourself and on their background, personality, gender and sex. Using first name terms can often lead to a more relaxed atmosphere but in some cases you might need to address a pupil more formally.

Physical contact should be avoided wherever possible as it can be misunderstood and resented. Sit in a position where the pupil cannot accidentally touch you. For example, it could be embarrassing if your leg gets in the way of the handbrake, and the pupil touches it.

PATIENCE – Just because you may have told the pupil something many times, don't assume that it will be remembered. Be patient! You should be sympathetic and try to rephrase your explanations so that they may be more readily understood. There are different degrees of impatience. These range from sarcastic comments, or tone of voice, and impatient body movements, to total loss of self-control and open hostility towards the pupil.

It will do you no good to get angry in a situation where your pupil already knows that they have done something wrong. Being patient will assist in the learning process by keeping the pupil calm. You will find that this will also lead to a greater degree of cooperation and effort.

TACT – You need to display an awareness of the correct thing to do or say so as to avoid giving offence to a pupil. This requires an intuitive understanding of the needs and feelings of your pupil.

THE ABILITY TO INSPIRE CONFIDENCE – Your own enthusiasm will be reflected in the efforts made by your pupils. They will not normally work as hard if you appear to be bored or disinterested.

Encouragement should be given when needed, and praise given where credit is due. This is just as important as the correction of errors, as it will develop the pupil's confidence and inspire further effort.

RECAP – At the end of the lesson you should give your pupil some FEEDBACK on how the lesson has gone, what has been learnt, where possible improvements have taken place and any weak points which will require further instruction.

Look forward to the next lesson, indicating which topics will be covered, suggesting any relevant reading material that needs to be studied.

It can be useful to show the SE that you keep records of your pupils's progress and weaknesses. This will show that you are monitoring and assessing what has been covered and what has still to be learnt, and that your pupils are kept informed of their progress. This will also prepare you for the introduction of student 'logbooks'.

GETTING THE BEST GRADING

Preparation for the Check Test is most important if you wish to get the best possible grading. If you are in doubt over any instructional points you should consider taking some training to update your teaching skills. It might be worthwhile to do this anyway, rather than leave it too late and be told that your methods are outdated, and your SE grades you as 'sub-standard'.

Don't be tempted to use a pupil whose driving is very good – if you select one who needs little or no instruction you will not be able to demonstrate your teaching ability effectively. Using a pupil who has plenty of room for improvement will allow you to bring about some progress during the lesson. This should be one of your prime objectives on the Check Test.

Make sure that your pupil is properly briefed about the Check Test – what it is, who will be conducting it and what the procedure will be. Draw up an appropriate lesson plan and make sure that both the pupil and the SE are aware of the objectives for the lesson. Don't try to cram too many things into the one lesson. It is better to bring about some improvement in one aspect of driving than try to improve the overall ability of the pupil in all aspects.

Your instruction should be based on the lesson plan and the pupil's ability but be prepared to modify the objectives if necessary. Flexibility is the key to good instruction.

> *Brief your pupils at the start of the lesson, give feedback during the lesson if appropriate and make time to give a thorough debriefing and some feedback at the end. Involve your pupils as much as possible by using Q&A techniques and inviting questions from them.*

Try to avoid retrospective instruction. Be positive and identify any faults made, analysing their causes. Think about and discuss solutions, getting your pupil to work with you in improving any weak points.

Self-assessment before the Check Test

In assessing your overall instructional ability, the SE will in particular be considering your:

- individual characteristics as an instructor;
- instruction/teaching ability; and
- fault identification, analysis, and correction.

Before you take the Check Test analyse your own performance in these three areas.

Instructor characteristics

Clarity – Are your verbal instructions clear and articulate?
Enthusiasm – Do you sound enthusiastic about the subject and the progress the pupil is making?

Encouragement – Do you encourage the pupil as often as you should?

Manner – Are you friendly and able to put your pupil at ease?

Patience and tact – Do you sound impatient or show your impatience or lack of tact when the pupil gets something wrong?

Instructional techniques

Recap at the start of the lesson – Do you remind the pupil what was covered and achieved in the previous lesson?

Objectives – Do you clearly define and state the objectives for the lesson you are giving?

Level of instruction – Do you match the level of instruction to suit the needs and ability of each pupil?

Instructions given – Are they easy for the pupil to understand or are they sometimes ambiguous?

Language – Do you keep it simple, avoiding jargon and technical words that the pupil may not understand?

Q&A technique – Do you use questions effectively and invite questions from your pupil?

Feedback – Do you give it yourself and gain it from your pupil and, if so, do you act properly on it?

Recap at the end of the lesson – Does your pupil get out of the car knowing what has been achieved and feeling good?

Use of dual controls – Do you use the dual controls only when necessary or do you use them excessively?

Fault assessment

Fault identification – Do you always accurately identify faults made by your pupils?

Fault analysis – Do you analyse the faults made in such a way that your pupils understand what has gone wrong and how to put it right?

Remedial action – Do you make sure that your pupils have the opportunity to remedy any faults made?

Timing of fault – Do you assess faults made while they are still fresh in the pupil's mind, or do you leave it so late that your pupil cannot recall the situation?

If you are in any doubt about any of these check points, you should refer to earlier chapters in this book which cover them in more detail.

Some dos and don'ts

DO

- Prepare in advance – your car, the pupil, the lesson plan.
- Take account of any recommendations the SE made in any previous Check Test.
- Brief both the pupil and the SE.
- Pitch the instruction at an appropriate level.
- Use a two-way Question and Answer technique.
- Ensure that some learning takes place during the lesson.
- Identify, analyse and correct any faults.
- Use encouragement when needed and praise when deserved.
- Sum up at the end of the lesson and look forward to the next one.

DON'T

- Choose a pupil for their good driving ability.
- Use retrospective correctice instruction.
- Involve the SE in the lesson.
- Try to carry out a mock test.

You owe it to yourself to obtain the best possible grading. If you are at all worried about the standard of your instruction, then consider taking some specialist training to prepare you for the Check Test. This should be done well before the date so that you have time to improve your PTS.

THE RESULT

At the end of the Check Test the SE will have assessed your instruction. You will be advised of the result and your overall performance will be discussed in order to assist you in bringing about any necessary improvement.

If you have passed, you will be given a grade – 4, 5, or 6. If you are given a grade 4 this means that your instruction was only adequate. A grade 5 means that your instruction was good; a grade 6 indicates that the instruction observed was very good indeed.

At this stage you will be given the opportunity to discuss with the SE anything that you do not understand about the grading given or any recommendations that are made. These recommendations are designed to help you to build on your strengths and correct any weak points.

The grade awarded will determine how soon you will be asked to take the next Check Test. As a rough guide, you could normally expect to be seen again within two years if you achieved a grade 4, three years if you achieved a grade 5, or four years if you achieved a grade 6. For a full analysis of the grades refer to *The Driving Insturctor's Handbook*.

If you have failed, the SE will tell you how soon you will be required to retake the test. Any grade below 4 will require a further Check Test fairly soon. If you get a grade 3 you will normally be seen within three months; with a grade 2 you will be seen within two months. In each case, the SE will expect to see a significant improvement on the next Check Test. You should seriously consider taking retraining to bring your instruction up to the required standard.

Should you be given a grade 1 on your Check Test, this would indicate that your instruction is considered to be dangerous. In this case, a second test will be arranged very quickly. If your instruction is still considered dangerous, you would not normally be allowed a third attempt.

If there is anything the SE has explained that you don't fully understand, the chances are you will find more detail about it in this book. Use the Contents pages and the Index to find the appropriate section.

Failing that, you can always telephone the SE on a Friday morning if you have any difficulty in understanding or implementing the recommendations made.

If you fail a further Check Test with an SE, you will then be required to take another test with a more senior examiner. At this stage, if your instruction has not improved, the Registrar will consider removing your name from the Register of ADIs.

In all cases of failure, the SE will confirm in writing what aspects of instruction were considered inadequate or wrong.

Irrespective of any recommendations that your SE makes, you should always ask yourself:

- Was there anything more I could have done to make my teaching more effective so as to bring about more learning for my pupil?
- How can I go about implementing the suggestions made by the SE?
- Would I benefit from investing in some retraining?

Finally, GOOD LUCK when you next take your Check Test!

9

Training for the ADI exams

Preparing for the three tests has already been dealt with earlier in this book. This chapter is designed to help you decide on the training plan that will best suit your particular needs. It may help if you refer again to *The Official DSA Guide for Driving Instructors* to remind yourself of the full syllabus and the stringent requirements of this exam.

THE IMPORTANCE OF GOOD TRAINING

Today's driving instructor has to be an effective teacher – not just someone who rides around telling people where to go and what to do.

This means that you will need to be able to teach new drivers to understand the whys and wherefores involved in safe driving.

It is vital to remember that, although you are initially training for an examination, you are also preparing yourself for a job that involves potential danger. You will therefore need to commit yourself to having sufficient training in order to achieve both of these objectives.

The pass rate for the theory test is around 50 per cent. This should emphasise the need to study the recommended reading materials thoroughly in order to gain a proper understanding of the principles involved in safe driving and effective teaching.

For the ADI driving test, the pass rate is around 45 per cent. Again this figure would point to candidates not being thoroughly prepared. Too many candidates are not fully aware of the high standard of driving skills required.

The pass rate for the test of instructional ability is even lower, at around 30 per cent. This would seem to emphasise even further the fact that far too many candidates are ill-prepared. There are two main reasons for this high failure rate:

1.   Many look for cheap options and use trainers with little expertise. Your local instructor may be extremely good at L-driver training and have an excellent pass rate. However, training to teach requires totally different skills from teaching driving.

2.   Too many candidates have insufficient training and are not properly prepared, neither for the exam nor for the job.

A good course should not only include those subjects on which you might be assessed during your Part 3 test, but also provide you with training in other important topics included in the *official syllabus for learners*. These include:

● dual carriageways;

● roundabouts;

● rural roads and other driving situations not included in the Part 3 syllabus.

Through your studies for the test of theory and preparation for the ADI driving test, you may know the subject well and are able to apply the correct driving rules and procedures effectively in all situations. However, putting over that knowledge to new drivers in a way that will encourage learning to take place is a totally different matter.

> *To learn how to become an effective driving instructor you will need plenty of expert guidance.*

A good trainer will be able to teach you how to:

● find out what your pupil already knows;

- establish a baseline for each lesson;
- pitch the instruction at a level to suit the pupil's ability and personality;
- analyse any problem areas;
- give positive and constructive advice;
- allow for practising the correct routines;
- teach *safe driving for life*.

You will also need to be taught to cope with the complexities of teaching a wide range of subjects, in a moving classroom and with different abilities, personalities and weaknesses.

Think of your training fees as being an investment towards a new career. Don't opt for what might appear to be the cheapest and shortest course. *THERE ARE NO SHORT CUTS!*

SELECTING A COURSE THAT SUITS YOU

The course you select will obviously depend on your particular circumstances. However, before making your final decision, you should bear in mind that the structure of the exam, together with the waiting time for practical appointments, means that it is not a process that you can rush through within a couple of months.

To be realistic, if everything goes well and you pass each element at the first attempt, it will take you *at least* six months from beginning your studies to the registration stage. If you opt for the *Trainee Licence* scheme, then the process could take much longer if you are to gain the full benefit of the six-month licence period.

TRAINING OPTIONS

The three main options are:

1. part-time studies and training organised around current work commitments;
2. an intensive course that involves classroom studies and in-car work for all three elements of the exam;
3. studying for and passing the theory test, training for the driving and instructional tests, and taking out a six-month *trainee licence*.

PART-TIME STUDYING AND PRACTICAL TRAINING

This option best suits those who are in full- or part-time employment and wish to fit in their training around these commitments.

As explained earlier in this book, the syllabus for the theory test is very comprehensive and you need to be prepared to devote quite a lot of your spare time to your studies. The more thoroughly you understand the principles covered in this syllabus, the better prepared you will be for your practical training.

A regularly updated distance-learning programme, covering the entire syllabus (and one that is used by numerous training establishments throughout the United Kingdom) is available from Margaret Stacey. Information can be found on her Web site: www.autodriva.co.uk.

It is most effective to overlap your preparation for the three elements of the exam. Whilst learning the rules and regulations for driving and teaching in readiness for the theory test, your trainer will ensure that you are putting them into practice when you drive. You will also see at first hand how your trainer applies the teaching principles in preparing you for the two practical tests.

Establishments offering this type of part-time individual course normally charge you per each training element. This means, therefore, that you will be able to spread the cost over the duration of your training period.

Everyone has a different rate of learning and training needs vary from one individual to another. Unlike many of the intensive courses, which usually stipulate within the fee a specific amount of training per exam element, the part-time course means that the amount of training will be structured to meet your personal needs.

However, you may prefer to share a course so that you can experience interaction with other trainees.

INTENSIVE COURSES

There are many different types of intensive course available. These vary in structure and duration. The syllabus should be compatible with the DSA's requirements for the ADI exam and also with their *recommended syllabus for learners*.

Much of the work is carried out in the classroom. This normally includes studies for the theory test and tuition on the principles involved in good driving and how to structure driving lessons.

Practical training is usually carried out on a ratio of one tutor to two trainees.

The DSA recommends this to be a maximum and some people might benefit from watching as well as being actively involved. If there are three trainees to one trainer, learning will become less effective and, obviously, less time will be available to deal with any specific problems you may have.

No matter what your personal needs may be, the course fee may be restrictive on how much training you are allowed for each element of the exam. You may be required to pay for any supplementary training you need.

Planning for any additional training to be outside the 'intensive course' timetable may also sometimes be difficult, as the establishment will normally have to schedule this at a time that suits you and another trainee.

If you opt for this method of training, you may be required to pay part or all of the fees in advance. Remember, there are absolutely no guarantees that you will pass all three tests. You should be made fully aware of the costing structure and whether or not you will be entitled to any refund of fees should you not be able, for any reason, to complete the course.

Practice

With both of the foregoing methods of training you can get practice instructing friends or relatives. You must remember, however, that you are not allowed to take payment in any form. You cannot even take money for fuel or any other costs incurred. If you are attending a course with other trainees, you may wish to practice with each other.

If you select either of the above methods of training, and:

- listen to the advice given;
- have as much tuition as is recommended;
- tuition is of sufficiently high quality; and
- your trainer is experienced in ADI training and expert at role play.

you should be able to qualify independently of the *Trainee Licence* system.

THE TRAINEE LICENCE

This system allows you to get practice with paying learners while preparing for the Part 3.

You have to pass both the theory and driving tests before being considered for a *trainee licence*. (You can do this through either of the above two methods.) You then have to be sponsored by a qualified instructor, whose driving school address will be shown on the licence. This instructor should take responsibility for your training and supervision.

The *trainee licence* option will normally entail you in taking up a full- or part-time position with a driving school. There are various schemes available, many of which include taking up a franchise with one of the larger schools.

If you already have a job, you need to consider this option very carefully. You will probably have to give it up in order to work in line with the conditions set out by the sponsoring driving school. (Remember, there are no absolute guarantees that you will pass the Part 3.)

Before you can apply for a trainee licence you must receive 40 hours training from a qualified ADI. You must receive training in all the following subjects:

1. Explaining the controls of the vehicle, including the use of the dual controls.

2. Moving off.

3. Making normal stops.

4. Reversing, and while doing so entering limited openings to the right or to the left.

5. Turning to face the opposite direction, using forward and reverse gears.

6. Parking close to the kerb using forward and reverse gears.

7. Using mirrors and explaining how to make an emergency stop.

8. Approaching and turning corners.

9. Judging speed, and making normal progress.

10. Road positioning.

11. Dealing with road junctions.

12. Dealing with crossroads.

13. Dealing with pedestrian crossings.

14. Overtaking, meeting and crossing the path of other road users, allowing adequate clearance.

15. Giving correct signals.

16. Comprehension of traffic signs, including road markings and traffic control signals.

17. Method, clarity, adequacy and correctness of instruction.

18. General manner.

19. Manner, patience and tact in dealing with pupils.

20. Ability to inspire confidence in pupils.

You should bear in mind that **you are responsible for making sure that you get this training**. A record of it must be kept on the form ADI 21T. This has to be signed by yourself and your trainer and sent in with your application for the licence.

Under the *Trainee Licence* scheme, you are not allowed to advertise yourself as a fully qualified instructor and you must abide by one of the following conditions:

(a) Twenty per cent of all of the lessons you give must be supervised by your sponsoring ADI. A record must be kept on the form ADI 21S of all of the lessons you give and the supervision received. This form must be signed by yourself and your sponsor and returned to the DSA as soon as the licence expires.

or

(b) You must receive a minimum additional 20 hours training covering all the foregoing list of topics. This training must take place within three months of issue of the licence, or before you take your first attempt at the Part 3, whichever is the sooner. A record of this training must be kept on the form ADI 21AT and must be sent to the DSA before the end of the three-month period, or presented to the examiner conducting your Part 3 test if this is the sooner. At least 25 per cent of this must be in-car training, with a maximum instructor: trainee ratio of no more than two trainees to one ADI.

If option (b) is selected and you fail at your first attempt, an additional five hours' training must be taken before you will be allowed to take a further test. This also applies if you fail at the second attempt. A declaration that you have had this extra training must be signed by you and your sponsoring ADI and handed to your examiner on the day of the test. If you do not do this, then the test will be cancelled and you will lose the fee.

For full information about the legal requirements of this system, refer to the *ADI 14 – Your road to becoming an Approved Driving Instructor* (Car) and *The Official DSA Guide for Driving Instructors*.

SELECTING YOUR TRAINER

Selecting a good trainer is your first step to achieving your goal of becoming an effective driving instructor. Good trainers are able to help you:

- understand the importance of the instructor's role and of teaching safe driving skills;
- develop your attitude and skills so that you will become a proficient and responsible instructor;

- communicate effectively;
- prepare thoroughly for all three parts of the ADI examination;
- learn to teach effectively in the car, and in the classroom where applicable;
- construct an effective and flexible training programme to suit the needs of individual pupils;
- seek further training for personal development;
- with advice on ADI and road safety organisations;
- prepare for running your driving school business.

ROLE PLAY

Many candidates for the Part 3 experience difficulty in dealing with the role-play situation. It is unnatural to try to treat someone as a learner when you know they are an extremely proficient driver. One of the most important assets of the good trainer, therefore, is, whilst maintaining safety throughout, having the ability to role play effectively. A good trainer should be able to:

- simulate drivers at all levels of experience and ability;
- play the role of people with different characteristics, for example: shy and retiring; forthright; argumentative; indifferent;
- introduce a wide variety of driver errors relating to the different topics under instruction;
- do only what they are told to do – in spite of an instruction being incorrect, a good trainer must go against instinct and do only as instructed, for example when given an instruction to select a gear before being told to push down the clutch;
- create opportunities for you to make positive correction through not responding properly to the road and traffic situation.

Experiencing the role-play situation in a wide variety of situations should give you a good grounding for dealing with your examiner.

There are currently no mandatory qualifications for the trainers of driving instructors. It is accepted, however, that qualifications other than that of ADI can be helpful. These include:

- AEB/DIA Diploma in Driving Instruction. (Preparing for this qualification gives the prospective ADI trainer a good foundation of knowledge.)

- Cardington Special Driving Test. (In seeking personal development through taking this test, the trainer is able to maximise efficiency and performance by training Part 2 candidates to a similar style and standard.)

- City & Guilds 7307 Further & Adult Education Teaching Certificate. (A qualification particularly useful for those engaged in classroom teaching.)

- City & Guilds 7254 Certificate in Training Competence. (Most appropriate for those preparing candidates for the practical elements of the ADI exam.)

- NVQ in driving instruction. (The role-play aspect of this qualification is extremely useful for ADI trainers.)

- NVQ Assessor's Award. (Useful for those mentoring ADIs for the NVQ in driving instruction.)

- ADI National Joint Council Tutor's Certificate. (A good foundation for those involved in the training of new instructors and the updating of ADIs preparing for the Check Test.)

- MSA GB Tutor's Certificate. (Similar advantages to the above qualification.)

TRAINING ESTABLISHMENTS

There is currently no mandatory register for instructor training and there are many training establishments throughout the United Kingdom offering a variety of different types of course. Many of these are independent and offer excellent training.

There is, however, a voluntary scheme that many establishments have opted to join. This is ORDIT – the Official Register of Instructor Training. It is administered by the DSA and regulated by the industry.

To gain registration, an establishment has to undergo an inspection carried out by DSA personnel. Following this, an inspection report is considered by the Management Committee. This is made up of elected representatives from current ORDIT establishments and representatives from the following organisations:

- AA the Driving School;
- ADINJC (Approved Driving Instructors' National Joint Council);
- BSM (The British School of Motoring);
- DIA (The Driving Instructors' Association);

- DISC (The Driving Instructor's Scottish Council);
- MSA GB (The Motor Schools' Association of Great Britain).

Information regarding ORDIT can be obtained from the DSA in Nottingham and a full list of registered establishments is contained within the ADI 14 Starter Pack.

10

Continuous personal development

Some driving instructors are perfectly happy to devote their career to teaching learner drivers. However, there is a need for all instructors to continually seek ways of developing and improving both their teaching skills and level of professionalism.

If you are looking for more variety, you could think about further developing your practical teaching skills in order not only to improve your teaching skills, but also to expand your potential market.

By developing the PTS and other transferable personal skills in this book, you will improve your self-assurance and confidence. Situations that once seemed very daunting, such as your Check Test, should become enjoyable and you may feel that you are now ready to look for new challenges.

CPD – *continuous personal* (or *professional*) *development* is now even more important in a world that is very competitive.

For some instructors, however, the specific personal benefits will be more important than the wider career implications.

Many driving instructors fall into this category. They sometimes are not keen to work with others and prefer to be left alone to 'do their own thing'. Many do not even choose to join any ADI association. It is probable that one of the reasons they chose to become driving instructors in the first place was that they would be left to work alone, at their own pace and in their own way.

This chapter should help you to develop your personality by improving the following:

● *Personal skills*
  – *Assertive skills*
  – *Affective skills*
  – *Reflective skills*
● *Problem-solving skills*
● *Decision-making skills*

The development of all these skills will greatly enhance your teaching ability by making you more 'personable'. This, when combined with the other PTS, should result in you receiving more recommendations from existing and past pupils.

Your personality profoundly influences how you behave, react and feel towards others and towards difficult situations. How other people react and respond to you will be determined partly by your personality and the confidence that you display to others.

This is particularly so in the environment of driving instruction where you are dealing with others on a one-to-one basis or in small groups. Your pupils, in particular, will look to you for advice and help.

People with similar personalities tend to work together more harmoniously. You should therefore try to adapt your personality to match that of each individual pupil.

Remember, to be able to teach Mary how to drive, you firstly have to know all about driving and, secondly, you have got to know something about Mary!

> *Knowing and understanding your personality, and being able to modify it to match that of the people you are dealing with, will help you to interact more effectively with them.*

Some instructors do this intuitively, without having to think about it. Others have to work at improving the technique, just as they do with the other PTS.

Listed below are a number of words which describe various personality characteristics. Read through the list, ticking those which you recognise in yourself. Put a cross beside those that you think do not describe yourself.

Adaptable	Aggressive	Aloof	Ambitious
Amiable	Argumentative	Assertive	Caring
Cheerful	Confident	Considerate	Creative
Decisive	Defensive	Dependable	Determined
Easy-going	Emotional	Enthusiastic	Extrovert
Fickle	Flexible	Forceful	Friendly
Gregarious	Hard-working	Honest	Humorous
Inconsiderate	Mild-mannered	Obstinate	Open-minded
Orderly	Over-cautious	Persistent	Reliable
Reticent	Self-conscious	Shy	Sincere
Systematic	Tactful	Tenacious	Trustworthy

When you have done this, look at the personality traits you have ticked and assess how you come across to your pupils. How do your friends think of you? Do they see you in the same way as your pupils do? Do they see you in the same way as you see yourself? Do they see you as being aloof, inconsiderate and over-cautious, or do they see you as being friendly, considerate and confident?

Ask three close friends to write down three words each which they think sum up your personality, then compare it with your own list and see how well they match up.

Consider how your pupils think of you. Do they see you in the same way as your friends do? This analysis should help you to see yourself as others see you.

• PERSONAL SKILLS

Personality development is dependent upon improving your assertive, affective and reflective skills.

The development of these will in turn help you to strengthen two other skills which you use every day of your working life: PROBLEM-SOLVING SKILLS and DECISION-MAKING SKILLS.

In Chapter 4 we mentioned that you must be able to persuade pupils to do whatever it is that you would like them to do in the way that you want them to do it. Persuasion is not only necessary when dealing with pupils' control of the vehicle and road procedure but also when handling other problems which may arise from time to time, such as unreasonable requests from pupils.

In dealing with these situations you need to use ASSERTIVE SKILLS and AFFECTIVE SKILLS.

Assertive skills

Assertiveness is the art of using clear and direct communication in order to get people to do what you want them to. When dealing with pupils you will need to be assertive, but in a friendly and sensitive way, sometimes with safety in mind. Being assertive enables you to:

- be direct and ask for what you want;
- say 'no' clearly and firmly without causing offence and embarrassment; and
- take responsibility or control, sometimes against the wishes of your pupil.

Some instructors are naturally assertive while others are more reticent and find it difficult to say 'No', or refuse unreasonable requests. If you are a non-assertive individual you need to realise that being assertive does not involve aggression, but simply firmness.

There are many situations in which you will need to be assertive, for example in asking a pupil to do something that they might see as being unreasonable:

'Julie, I would like you to consider postponing your test!'

coping with the refusal of a request:

'If you don't postpone the test Julie, I will not be able to let you use the school car as you are not safe!'

refusing a request yourself:

'I'm sorry John, but you are not yet ready to put in for the driving test. Your driving needs to be more consistent.'

apologising:

'I'm sorry that you feel you want to change instructors, but if I let you go on test when you are still unsafe the examiner will not be very pleased and you may have an accident. If you don't trust my judgement, then perhaps it *would* be better if you found another instructor!'

The easiest way to be assertive without causing offence is to be: Factual, Positive, Persuasive and Persistent.

One way of helping to overcome difficult situations is to clearly state your 'trading terms' on the pupil's appointment card. For example:

Cancellations – Unless 24 hours' notice is given, lessons will be charged for.

The school cannot be held responsible for postponement of the test due to bad weather or illness of the examiner.

Your instructor is one of the best-trained in the profession and you should be guided by him/her regarding your readiness for the test. Your instructor will advise you when you should apply for the driving test.

The school car is available for driving tests, at the discretion of the instructor and subject to regular lessons being maintained.

In the interests of road safety, use of the school car for a driving test may be refused if, at the discretion of the instructor, the pupil is considered to be unsafe.

The simple provision of the above on the appointment card will lessen the chances of arguments of this nature by adding weight to your words. In the eyes of the pupil the decision becomes 'company policy' and not just a whim of yours. The fact that you may be 'the company' is neither here nor there.

Being assertive in a sensitive way will be easier to achieve if you develop your AFFECTIVE SKILLS.

Affective skills

AFFECTIVE in this context refers to your feelings and emotions, your attitudes and values, and how these 'affect' your interpersonal relationships.

Often, how successfully you deal with people and problems is determined by how you are feeling at the time, and your attitude towards the person or problem you are dealing with.

When dealing with other people, always try to:

- Treat them with respect. Even though you may be feeling low, do not release your frustrations on them. Try to control any 'mood swings' you may have.

- Be sensitive to their feelings and problems. Try not to offend people by what you say and how you say it. Get their side of the story and listen carefully to what they say. Respect their feelings but help them to see your side too.

- Be polite. Do not be rude or expect them to be servile. Treat them as you would wish to be treated yourself.

- Be sympathetic. Show concern for their well-being. Learn to pick up both verbal and non-verbal signals which may indicate their concern. Make time to find out what the cause of their concern is and provide sympathy and support when needed.

Look for and consider alternative solutions. For example, 'Could you manage to fit in some extra lessons in order to correct the problems you are having with emerging at junctions? Perhaps you could get some extra practice with your family.'

When confrontations of this nature do occur, always analyse the way you dealt with the situation. Ask yourself whether you did everything possible to work out alternative solutions to the problem. How did the pupil react to your handling of the situation?

You are likely to learn more from your mistakes than you will from your successes and the experience gained will help you to overcome similar problems in the future!

Your development of problem-solving skills (covered later in this chapter) will lessen the likelihood of you facing these types of situations.

Reflective skills

REFLECTIVE SKILLS can be used first of all to evaluate how your personality might be modified to make you more personable, and secondly to measure how well your PTS are developing.

When you reflect upon your current activities and interests, so as to be able to build on your strengths and improve your weaknesses, you need to be objective and use a systematic approach.

Only by painting yourself a clear picture of your character and personality will you be able to assess where your strengths lie and your weaknesses exist.

In this section we will be showing you how to use your reflective skills to develop your personality. As a starting point you need to reflect upon:

● current activities (other than giving lessons); and

● other interests and hobbies.

Current activities

To evaluate your current activities so as to establish where your strengths lie, begin by listing those activities that you frequently undertake. Try to be objective when completing the table, an example of which is given here.

Column one shows the ACTIVITY; column two shows the SKILLS REQUIRED; and column three shows how you RATE your ability in using the skills which are required. Use a bi-polar marking system similar to that used by the SE/ADI on the Check Test: 1 – being not competent in your use of the skill in question; 2 – having some competence; 3 – being fairly competent; 4 – being very competent; 5 – being expert at using the skill.

Activities	*Skills required*	*Rating*
Involvement at local ADI association meetings	Working with groups Leading others Conversational skills Planning events Asscrtiveness Affectivc skills	
Attending local SEs meetings	Note-taking skills Listening skills Thinking skills Questioning skills	
Parent/teachers association or other committee work	Committee skills Communication skills Negotiating skills	

Other interests and hobbies

Like your work activities, your interests and hobbies also give you an insight into how well you use your personal skills. By analysing what you like doing, and the skills involved, you can shed light on your potential capabilities.

For example, if you enjoy playing football it might be because you get pleasure from competing against others (an enterprising skill), that you like to study other players' styles of play (requiring assessment skills), or that it gives you a sense of achicvement in trying to improve your performance (a personal skill).

Your interest in football may be less in the game itself and the result of the match than in the satisfaction you derive from playing the game.

List your interests and hobbies with those you most enjoy at the top and those you least enjoy at the bottom. In the second column, state explicitly the skills you use successfully in each of the interests, and in the third column give an evaluation of your skill – 1 being low, 5 being high.

For example, you might write something like this:

Rank order of interests	Skills required	Rating
1 Playing cards	Intellectual skills	4
	Verbal communication skills	2
	Reading body language	5
2 Reading novels	Reading skills	5
	Intellectual skills	3
3 Windsurfing	Dexterity skills	5
	Physical skills	5

Taking the above example, a picture emerges of an individual with interests that require little interaction with others. The skills that have been identified and assessed are very much INTRAPERSONAL rather than INTERPERSONAL. This would indicate that in order to develop a more balanced portfolio of skills, this person needs to seek interests that involve much more interaction with other people, such as team sports, activity clubs, local ADI associations or advanced driving organisations.

Problem-solving skills

In driving instruction, because of the continually changing situation, problem solving often needs to be carried out without the usual amount of time one has when solving problems in other environments.

When problems do arise, decisions often have to be taken immediately, sometimes with safety in mind.

Solving problems usually involves transferring knowledge and understanding stored in the long-term memory of new situations.

The good instructor will, if time allows, work with the pupil to solve the problem. The function of the instructor is to 'guide' the pupil towards solving the problem, presenting alternatives for consideration, and asking thought-provoking questions which will help the pupil to shed some light on the cause and cure.

If your pupils can, with your help, solve problems, they will be better able to understand why the problem arose in the first place, and how similar situations could be prevented in the future.

A systematic approach of following a series of stepping stones, should help pupils to identify the different options available, and eventually lead to the most feasible solution to problems.

If any of the steps are missed out, then it is unlikely that the best solution will be achieved. As each problem will be slightly different from the last, not all problems can be treated alike.

You must use your critical-thinking skills to ensure that the pupil considers all the options, arrives at the best solution, and successfully implements that solution.

Problem solving invariably precedes DECISION MAKING.

Decision-making skills

The purpose of PROBLEM SOLVING is to discover what caused a particular situation, so that you may use the knowledge to DECIDE exactly how to deal with it.

A key element in DECISION MAKING is that of ASSESSING and BALANCING risk.

For example, a partly trained pupil is approaching a traffic light which has been showing green for some time. Following your instructions, the pupil slows the car down to such a speed that it can be stopped if necessary. In normal circumstances, your car is just coming up to the line and the traffic light changes to amber. You know that the pupil could, and should, stop at the line, but there is a big lorry travelling much too close behind you. It's DECISION TIME!

You need to BALANCE the risk and because you don't have time to consult with your pupil, you probably say something like 'Keep going!' or 'Don't stop!' Had you said nothing then your pupil would probably have stopped suddenly with disastrous consequences.

In this sort of situation, where you have to override a pupil's decision, you would then need to stop somewhere safe and discuss what happened with your pupil. You will then need to explain to the pupil why their decision was over-ridden by you.

The usual steps in the decision-making process are:

1. specifying your aims;
2. reviewing the different factors;
3. determining the possible courses of action;
4. making the decision; and
5. implementing the decision.

This is fine under normal circumstances and when making business decisions for example, but when you are travelling along the road and situations are developing quickly, you need to simplify the process to:

$$\text{LOOK} \Rightarrow \text{ASSESS} \Rightarrow \text{DECIDE} \Rightarrow \text{ACT}$$

> *Your job is to transfer to pupils, as soon as possible, the responsibility to make decisions. However, you must also be prepared to override these decisions to maintain safety.*

The sooner your pupils are making decisions for themselves, the sooner they will be ready to drive unaccompanied.

For most pupils, the first time they will ever drive 'unaccompanied' is on the driving test, where the examiner should not be giving any verbal assistance. Before this, a good way to introduce decision making to test pupils' ability to make decisions, is to let them drive home towards the end of the lesson, giving no instructions or directions, except where unplanned situations arise and safety is in question.

Everybody makes mistakes, and when bad decisions have been made, either by you or your pupil, they should be analysed. You will both learn more from your mistakes than you will from your good decisions!

Assessments

Because of the predominance in the driving school market of the training of new drivers, some ADIs allow themselves to be limited by this tradition. There are, however, many ways in which you could achieve a greater degree of variety in your work and a higher level of job satisfaction. You could consider extending the services you offer to include:

● assessments for drivers seeking employment;

● minibus training for teachers and group leaders;

● refresher training for older people who may have lost their confidence;

● drivers of company vehicles;

● those who have lost their licence through disqualification;

● drivers who would like to take an advanced test.

Your PTS in these cases are going to come in useful, as you will need to be able to adjust your training to suit many types of driver, each with a different personality and level of knowledge, skill and experience. Certainly most of them will have different attitudes.

Before embarking on such a project, it would be sensible to undertake some training through an ORDIT or other independent training organisation to make sure that your instruction is flexible enough to adapt to the different drivers.

Valid driving licence		Mirror(s) signal approach to junctions	
Eyesight test		(MSMPSL)	
Introduction to car and controls		Position/speed/awareness	
Pre-starting drill		– position vehicle correctly before turning	
Starting up and moving off		right/left	
Slowing down and stopping		– avoiding cutting right-hand corners	
Make proper use of the accelerator		Overtake/meet/cross path of/other vehicles	
clutch		safely	
gears		Position vehicle correctly during normal	
footbrake		driving	
handbrake		Allow adequate clearance to stationary	
steering		vehicles	
Move away/safely/under control		Take appropriate action at pedestrian	
Moving off up/down hill/at an angle		crossings	
Stop vehicle in an emergency		Select a safe position for normal stops	
promptly/under control		Show awareness and anticipation of the	
Reverse into a limited opening left or right		actions of/pedestrians/cyclists/drivers	
under control/with due regard to others		Approaching – roundabouts	
Make effective use of mirror(s) well before:		– crossroads	
Take effective rear observation well before:		– traffic lights	
– signalling		– pedestrian crossings	
– changing direction		– one-way streets	
– slowing down or stopping		Speed appropriate	
Give signals where necessary/correctly/in		Overtaking moving vehicles	
good time		Anticipation	
Take prompt and appropriate action on all:		Driving in heavy traffic	
– traffic signs		Pupil taking the initiative	
– road markings		More difficult manoeuvres	
– traffic lights		Highway Code questions	
– signals given by traffic controllers		Parking	
– other road users		Competence at junctions etc	
Exercise proper care in the use of speed		Speed/lane positioning in line with conditions	
Make progress by avoiding undue		Practice test requirements	
hesitancy		Ready for Test?	
– driving at speed appropriate to road/traffic		Post-test lessons	
conditions		Motorway driving	
Act properly at road junctions		Advanced Driving Test	

Progress chart

Feedback and reports

Although most driving instruction and assessment is conducted on a verbal basis, you need to be able to provide written feedback on progress. This will apply when the mandatory logbook for learners is introduced and also should you embark on the training and assessment of more experienced drivers. Any third party will undoubtedly require some form of report if they are paying for your services.

This feedback may take the form of:

● recording progress at the end of lessons in a logbook;

● providing more detailed reports to third parties.

To promote your image as a professional you should consider the following when writing reports:

● The style and language of writing should be matched to the person for whom you are preparing the report.

● Your writing should be grammatically correct.

● The report should be neatly presented, ihether it be written, typed or produced on your computer.

● Make sure you check through your report at least a couple of times before submitting it.

EVALUATING YOUR PTS

This section will show you how to evaluate your skills, achievements and satisfactions. This will assist you in deciding how best to continue your personal and career development. To be able to evaluate your PTS you must use your REFLECTIVE SKILLS because much of the work involved in developing your PTS has to be done by yourself.

> *You need to recognise your strengths, analyse your weaknesses and implement a self-development programme. This refletion process requires you to be objective and to use a systematic approach.*

You should consider the following:

● the PTS you are currently using;

● your achievements; and

● your satisfactions.

The PTS you are currently using

You need to draw up a 'master list' of PTS, similar to that given below, which you can use to analyse and evaluate your levels of competence and decide which of the skills you need to improve.

To analyse how well you are using your portfolio of PTS, mark against the list how well you think you are doing. Use the following rating scale to indicate your level of ability.

1 – Not very good and requiring considerable improvement.
2 – Some basic ability but with need for improvement.
3 – Not bad, but scope for improvement.
4 – Reasonably compctent, slight room for improvement.
5 – Highly competent, scope for fine tuning.

PTS used while giving driving lessons   *Your Skill Rating (1–5)*

Verbal communication
Giving instructions
Giving directions
Giving explanations
Use of visual aids
Giving demonstrations
Own driving ability
Transferring knowledge
Transferring understanding
Transferring attitudes
Skill training
Question and answer techniques
Giving feedback
Gaining feedback
Listening skills
General appearance
Using positive body language
Reading the body language of your pupils
Giving encouragement when needed
Giving praise when deserved
Affective skills
Assertive skills
Being patient
Being sympathetic
Sounding enthusiastic
Putting the pupil at ease
Problem-solving skills
Decision-making skills
Recapping at the start of the lesson

PTS used while giving driving lessons	*Your Skill Rating (1–5)*
Lesson planning	
Teaching by objectives	
Clearly stating the objectives of lessons	
Selling ideas and concepts	
Matching the level of instruction to the ability of the pupil	
Flexibility in being able to change the lesson plan if necessary	
Route planning	
Use of simple and unambiguous language	
Transferring responsibility to the pupil	
Fault recognition	
Fault analysis	
Fault correction	
Timing of fault recognition and analysis	
Use of verbal intervention	
Use of dual controls	
Testing skills	
Recapping at the end of the lesson	
Linking forward to the next lesson	
Setting tasks for in between lessons	
Use of role-play skills (if relevant)	

When you see a list of all the skills you use every day of your working life without even thinking about them, it will help you to realise just how important the job of teaching someone safe driving as a life skill really is. Perhaps we should all be charging more than we do for the services that we provide!

Verbal communication skills	*Rating (1–5)*
Use of different tones of voice when speaking	
Use of emphasis when speaking	
Use of figurative language	
Use of humour	
Use of pronunciation	
Use of pitch	

Non-verbal communication skills	*Rating (1–5)*
Use of positive body language	
Use of appropriate dress	
Interpreting the body language of the learner	
Listening skills	

Written communication skills   *Rating (1–5)*

Written feedback for pupils/trainees
Recording pupils'/trainees' progress
Promotional and business letters
Hand-outs
Design of visual aids

Personality development   *Rating (1–5)*

Assertive skills
Affective skills
Reflective skills
Problem-solving skills
Decision-making skills

Group-work skills   *Rating (1–5)*

Classroom management
Leading a group
Developing a group
Working in a group

If we say that a grade 4 or 5 is acceptable, and 3 or below is unacceptable, we now know which skills need to be developed.

A good starting point for improvement would be to re-read the sections in this book dealing with any of the above-mentioned skills for which you have given yourself 3 or less.

You will then need to exercise self-determination or consider seeking professional help to improve the areas of weakness which you have identified. At the end of each lesson analyse your performance to see whether you think you have made improvement.

Your achievements

Many driving instructors tend to measure their achievements against how many pupils they get through the driving test first time. For the instructor who is serious about personal and career development, we need to look a bit further than that.

Your achievements do not have to make the headlines, but may simply be successes about which you feel pleased.

A useful starting point would be to list all of your achievements that you consider are important. They need not be connected only with your job, but could include achievements in your social life. Emphasise those achievements that you found difficult to attain.

When you have completed your list, evaluating the PTS you have used in gaining the achievements will give you some insight into your strengths and weaknesses.

For example, your list could look something like this:

Achievement	*PTS used*	*Rating*
Teaching a deaf person to drive	Use of visual aids	5
	Demonstration skills	5
	Flexibility	5
	Patience	4
	Being sympathetic	4
	Setting between-lesson tasks	5
Winning the football competition	Teamworking	4
	Physical skills	5
Achieving a Grade 6 check test	Articulation	4
(The SE's comments should help	Enthusiasm	3
you to rate each component skill	Encouragement	4
used during the check test)	Friendliness	5
	Patience	5
	Self-confidence	4
	Objectives clear	5
	Level of instruction suitable	5
	Instructions easily understood	5
	Simple language used	4
	Q&A techniques	5
	Recap at the start	3
	Recap at the end	5
	Faults identified	5
	Fault analysis attempted	5
	Fault analysis correct	4
	Remedial action	4
	Timing of fault assessment	3
Cardington Grade A pass	Driving skills	5
(Special driving test)		

The person profiled above is able to accept pressure and to work well with others. To achieve examination/test success the individual must have prepared well, which required self-discipline. You could summarise this person as being determined and dedicated.

Your satisfactions

Your self-awareness will be enhanced by evaluating your satisfactions. Everyone obtains satisfaction from some activity in which they participate.

Listed below is a range of PTS. Against each skill you can indicate in the second column the level of satisfaction gained when using it. In the third column you can rate your skill level.

Your own list could look something like this:

PTS	Gain	Rating
Chairing meetings	satisfaction	4
Attending meetings	satisfaction	3
Leading others	satisfaction	4
Working with others	dissatisfaction	2
Taking decisions	satisfaction	3
Solving problems	satisfaction	5
Making formal presentations	dissatisfaction	1
Selling	dissatisfaction	2
Writing letters	dissatisfaction	2
Keeping accounts	dissatisfaction	2
Conversing with friends	satisfaction	5
Conversing with strangers	dissatisfaction	2
Using positive body language	satisfaction	4
Reading body language	satisfaction	5

Although the above list is not exhaustive or typical it may give you some ideas for compiling your own. By deciding whether or not you gain satisfaction by using your PTS you will gain insight into where some of your strengths lie and which weaknesses need to be overcome.

> By developing your weakest PTS and reflecting on your achievements and satisfactions, you will most certainly become a better driving instructor.

You are also likely to become more personable, which should result in you getting more recommendations and improving your social life as well.

Change and development do not come overnight, however, and you should treat each new business and social encounter as an opportunity to experiment, practise, experience and reflect. If you are doing the same thing now that you were doing five years ago, you are probably doing something wrong! Development is a lifelong challenge but one which is well worth accepting for those brave enough to try.

BASIC CAR MECHANICS

One of the topics included in the DSA's syllablus for learning to drive is 'Car controls, equipment and components'. Although, as a driving instructor, you do not need to know how every component in your car works, or how to carry out repairs, you should be able to teach your pupils some of the more basic principles and procedures.

Having even basic knowledge of how the car works should help your pupils develop vehicle sympathy. Showing them how to carry out routine checks and identify defects should also avoid unnecessary delays and breakdowns for them.

The Driving Instructor's Handbook contains a complete chapter on the car and you can use this as a reference source, along with your own vehicle handbook, when you are preparing your lesson plans.

Items which you could cover include:

- re-fuelling the car;
- checking oil, water and fluid levels;
- checking tyre pressures and condition;
- checking bulbs and replacing them;
- wheel changing;
- routine preventative maintenance.

If you have the appropriate level of knowledge and skills, you might even consider taking things a little further and teach the more enthusiastic new drivers basic maintenance and servicing requirements.

The way in which you teach this subject will depend entirely on whether you wish to cover it on an individual basis, or whether you wish to teach it to groups of pupils.

On a 'one-to-one' basis you can combine an educational re-fuelling stop with showing your pupils how to make the basic checks and bulb replacements. If you intend to go a little deeper into the subject and teach it in groups, you will need to either use your own garage or locate suitable premises where you will have the space to work in.

For more comprehensive coverage of car mechanics you might even consider hiring classroom facilities and obtaining models of different parts of the car to show how they work.

By helping your pupils to develop a sympathetic attitude towards the car they are more likely to drive economically and safely.

TEACHING IN THE CLASSROOM

Many driving instructors view teaching in the classroom as being pure theory training, and teaching in the car as practical instruction. This is largely due to the haphazard way in which driving instruction in this country has evolved over the years.

When teaching takes place in the car or in the classroom, there are both theoretical and practical components which should be covered by the teacher.

Some instructors already teach in adult education centres, instructor training centres or in secondary schools, giving pre-driver training. Teaching in the classroom can be more economical in preparing groups of pupils for their theory test.

Solo driving instructors should be able to band together to provide classroom facilities. The PTS in this book will be invaluable for your classroom work.

The teacher is responsible for managing the environment, the available resources and the instruction given, so that pupils may learn as effectively as possible.

In-class sessions should be made as practical as possible and linked to in-car practice. The following aspects will need to be borne in mind.

Teacher Activity

As the classroom teacher, you will need to:

- prepare the lesson plan;
- be punctual (allow time to check equipment);
- dress appropriately;
- ensure that any new students know your name;
- keep a register if the lesson is one of a series of lessons so that attendance and progress can be monitored; and
- deliver the lesson.

The classroom

You must give consideration to:

- size, lighting, heating, ventilation, provision of drinking water;
- seating arrangement (be prepared to rearrange the seating layout from time to time to avoid social cliques forming and to suit the activity you have planned);
- equipment needed for the lesson – power points, extension leads, window blinds etc; and

- health and safety requirements – fire extinguisher, fire certificate and details of fire drill, toilet/washing facilities, safety of electrical equipment and leads.

Teaching/visual aids

These will need to be checked before the lesson and may include:

- black-/whiteboards, flip charts, chalk, markers etc;
- overhead projectors and transparencies;
- slide projectors and slides;
- film projectors and films;
- charts, diagrams, magnetic boards, models etc; and
- pre-prepared handouts.

The following rules will assist you in using any of the above teaching/visual aids effectively:

- ACCURACY – Keep them factual and accurate.
- BREVITY – Keep them simple, avoiding unnecessary detail.
- CLARITY – Ensure that any lettering is big enough to be seen clearly.
- DELETION – Use them, then lose them – otherwise they become a distraction.
- EMPHASIS – Stress the key points.
- FEEDBACK – Carefully watch the students' reaction to the visual aids used so that you can evaluate their impact and effectiveness.

Teaching methods

You must avoid DOMINATING the lesson. Although teacher-centred learning can be useful in the early stages of learning or at the beginning of a given lesson, it will not assist the full development of the capabilities of your students.

Your learners will come to the classroom with needs and expectations which they hope to fulfil. These include:

- social needs, such as working in groups and competing with others;
- the desire to make progress and improve themselves; and
- the need to satisfy curiosity and perform tasks well.

The good teacher will make the learning PUPIL CENTRED by involving the students as much as possible and catering for the individual needs of each student where possible. This will be best achieved by you 'guiding' your students to reach their own conclusions, thus developing their abilities, building on strengths and improving any weaknesses.

Preparing lesson plans

When preparing a classroom lesson you should consider:

- an introduction;
- the development of the subject;
- a conclusion; and
- setting any homework.

An introduction
You should aim to get your class members working together as soon as possible. This will lessen the likelihood of social chatter, thus putting the amount of time available to best use.

The introduction should therefore be as short as possible, perhaps recapping on what was covered in the previous lesson by using the Q/A technique. The basic principles covering the aims and objectives of the lesson can then be outlined.

The development of the subject
This should actively involve the students in learning from the known to the unknown; building up knowledge progressively; moving from the simple to the more difficult.

Pupil activity could include: note taking; discussions; practising; Q/A sessions; stimulating games; role-play exercises; and a quiz or test.

You could deal with any homework set the previous week. Try to involve all members of the class, rather than marking their work individually. However, if this method is used, you should invite those members of the class who have done written or project work to leave with you for marking before the next lesson.

A conclusion
When concluding the lesson, you should consolidate any new information, knowledge or attitudes taught either by random Q/A sessions or by using a prepared list of questions.

This will allow you to evaluate your teaching, and how much learning has taken place. It should also reinforce the key points, stimulate the brighter students, and encourage the less able students to demonstrate what they have learnt.

Setting homework

Any homework set should be designed to consolidate the subject matter of the lesson given. Try to avoid making homework purely academic. Project work can be set to be dealt with during the next lesson, or homework could include some practical application of what has been taught, and what will be covered in the car.

Delivering the lesson

By using the PTS outlined in this book, you should be able to deliver a lesson to a class of students in an efficient and effective way.

Even if you are used to teaching groups, you will often feel nervous at the start of a lesson. This is perfectly normal but, as the lesson develops, your natural enthusiasm should take over and things should become more relaxed.

Provided the lesson has been prepared properly, and your notes are to hand, things should run reasonably smoothly.

A glass of water should be kept handy so that if you do 'dry up' you can take a quick drink and gather your thoughts. A packet of mints can also come in useful.

Try to make eye contact with each student in turn and speak to the class as if you are speaking to individuals. Don't be panicked by periods of silence – these can be useful and add impact and importance to what you are saying.

When using the blackboard or whiteboard, try not to cover up what you are writing or showing the class. Avoid talking to the class as you are writing on the board.

If you have a 'rollerboard' available it is sometimes useful to write your material on it before the lesson, as long as you do not roll it down and display it before you need it or forget to lose it after you've used it.

When asking questions use the POSE – PAUSE – POUNCE technique.

- POSE the question to the class generally;
- PAUSE for them to think about it; and
- POUNCE on the member of the class you wish to answer it.

Make sure that you spread your questions evenly around the group, giving everybody a chance to participate, especially the quieter members of the class.

After the lesson has finished analyse your own performance. If you can video the proceedings this will be very useful in evaluating how well you have delivered the lesson. Ask yourself:

- How well did I present myself to the class?
- Was the classroom laid out in an efficient way?
- Were the teaching/visual aids suitable for the lesson being given, and were they used effectively?
- Were the teaching methods used suitable for the group?
- How well did I prepare the lesson plan?
- Was the lesson delivered efficiently and effectively?

GROUP WORK SKILLS

Driving instructors often choose not to work in groups, preferring to teach on a one-to-one basis.

There may be, however, times in your life when you will have to work in a group, whether it be a group of local instructors, a local or national association, a group committee, or perhaps the parent/teachers' association of your children's school. In these situations you will be responsible for completing certain tasks which contribute to the effectiveness of the group as a whole.

The interactive skills which will be required in these situations are highly transferable and will be useful on many other occasions in both your business and personal life.

To work effectively within a group, the interactive PTS in this book will help you to:

- present yourself well to others;
- adopt an open attitude;
- be sensitive to the feelings and needs of others;
- allow an equal opportunity for all to contribute;
- accept criticisms;
- work with self-confidence; and
- acknowledge the role of the group leader.

In this section we will be dealing with: the nature of groups; leading a group; and developing groups.

The nature of groups

Forming groups goes back to our cave-dwelling days and is a natural process for most human beings. Most individuals seek the companionship and friendship of other people for a variety of reasons, both at work and in leisure.

Irrespective of whether a group is FORMAL or INFORMAL, OPEN or CLOSED, being a member of a group offers numerous advantages.

● Groups often accomplish tasks more effectively than individuals by allowing people to pool their resources and experience.

● By relying on the expertise of fellow members, individuals feel more secure when making decisions and taking action within the group.

● Groups provide emotional support which is not always available when working as an individual.

● Groups provide a sense of identity, thus increasing self-esteem and self-confidence and giving credibility to the individual.

● Members often choose to wear badges, ties, etc to display their allegiance to the group.

● A great sense of pride can come from being a member of a group, particularly where there are entry qualifications and requirements.

Leading a group

Some groups require one member to act as leader. The leader is usually responsible for ensuring that the group's activities assist in achieving its aims and objectives.

If the members of a group challenge its leadership, the group cannot function effectively. The group leader must therefore establish effective working relationships with most of the members of the group.

To successfully lead a group a number of responsibilities have to be accepted:

● Setting group aims and objectives.

● Agreeing mutually acceptable responsibilities for individual group members.

● Negotiating responsibilities with members.

● Consulting with group members on their progress in reaching individual targets.

● Motivating the group.

● Encouraging communication and co-operation within and outside the group.

● Solving problems and making decisions.

- Accepting the views, opinions and ideas of the group.
- Encouraging initiative within the group.
- Creating a harmonious working environment.
- Disciplining group members when necessary.

It is questionable whether good leaders are born or whether they can be trained. There is no doubt that by developing the communication skills in this book you will improve your leadership qualities. You will need to be assertive so as to be able to persuade group members to act in the way you consider best for the group.

> *Developing your interpersonal skills will help you to become an effective group leader even though you may not have been born one!*

Developing groups

Groups are much more easily developed if their members are not separated by long distances and have similar personalities and characteristics.

The more that attitudes are held in common, the better the group is likely to function.

Research has indicated that groups pass through four stages of development:

FORMING ⇒ STORMING ⇒ NORMING ⇒ PERFORMING

Forming – This is a 'testing the water' phase during which group members spend time establishing the reactions of other members to themselves and to the tasks and responsibilities to be carried out.

Forming is an important stage of group development in that it helps to set the standards of behaviour to which the group conforms.

Each group member tries to:

- create a favourable first impression by dress and manner;
- communicate with other members of the group;
- listen to what other members of the group are saying; and
- assert influence on the decision-making process.

Storming – Soon after formation, conflicts arise as group members argue about how power and status will be divided within the group. Some might think a leader should be elected. Some might seek a more democratic approach and others might want a combination of both approaches.

At this difficult stage of development you will need to:

- use your negotiating skills to help resolve conflicts;

- use your problem-solving skills, offering alternative solutions to resolve differences of opinion so that decisions may be made; and

- communicate effectively and assertively but try not to be too insistent on getting your own way – you may be able to bring other group members round to seeing things your way at a later stage.

Norming – As soon as the initial conflicts within the group are resolved, the group can settle down and begin to work efficiently. Individuals will accept their agreed responsibilities and procedures that need to be established are put in place. The group is now ready to undertake its tasks and activities.

Performing – Now that each group member is working for the good of the group, rather than for his or her own benefit, the group can concentrate on attaining its aims and objectives.

Not all groups will adhere exactly to the four stages outlined above but most will follow a similar development process. Understanding how groups work is important for members of any group. Groups are made up of individuals. They are dynamic. Each group member will influence the group by bringing knowledge, experience, skills, personality and attitude, all of which will help the group to function.

All the communication, personal and interpersonal skills in this book will assist you in working well within a group.

After each group encounter, assess your performance within the group. Ask yourself:

- Did I carry out my individual responsibilities/tasks to the best of my ability?

- Was my contribution in the best interests of the group, or did I let my individual aspirations get in the way?

- How can I best serve the interests of the group in the future?

DRIVING INSTRUCTOR TRAINING

When you have gained some experience as an ADI, have achieved a good Check Test grade, and your pupils have a consistently high pass rate, you might even consider becoming an instructor trainer or tutor.

To prepare yourself for this step up the ladder, you will need to:

- have a sound knowledge of the syllabus for the theory test and be able to provide the relevant study materials and support;
- drive at a consistently high standard and be able to adapt your practical work to suit drivers with much more experience; and
- be competent in the skills required to train people to teach;
- have undertaken some training with a specialist organisation.

By preparing for your ADI exam, you should be fully aware of the in-depth knowledge required for the Part 1 test of theory; and of the high standard of personal driving skills required for the driving test. However, training to instruct is different from teaching people to drive and you would need to develop many more PTS to progress into this field.

Some of the skills discussed, such as teaching in the classroom and working with groups, would certainly be beneficial. However, one of the most important parts of the *tutor's* job is being able to stimulate learners with differing abilities and personalities. *Role-play*, takes up a large percentage of the time spent training new instructors and you need to develop this PTS so that your simulation is credible.

If you do make the decision to become a tutor of ADIs, you should be able to confidently and effectively apply the PTS covered in this book.

You should seek advice and training from one of the specialist organisations before embarking on this more challenging branch of the driving instruction world.

What is role play?

In practice, role play mostly takes the form of short, unscripted playlets, involving two or more participants who take the part of different people in order to satisfy the specific training requirements. For example, in the case of driving instruction, the trainer plays the part of a learner at a specific level of ability and the trainee will be learning the role of the instructor.

The trainer should organise each playlet so that it simulates circumstances similar to those that the trainee will meet in everyday life as an instructor.

In order to prepare the trainee to deal with everyday situations with learners, different elements should be introduced so that the trainer is able to assess and improve on all aspects of the trainee's teaching skills.

For demonstration purposes, the trainer may sometimes choose to play the role of the instructor, with the trainee taking the part of the learner.

Why use role play?

Role play is a valuable technique, providing:

- participation;
- involvement;
- an opportunity for 'action learning';
- a safe environment in which to learn how to deal with situations that could, to an inexperienced ADI, be dangerous with a real learner.

In order to prepare the trainee to deal with different types of client, the trainer should simulate as many types of personality as possible. For example:

- the difficult customer, who 'knows it all';
- the slow learner, who needs lots of reinforcement and encouragement;
- the indifferent one, who doesn't want to put in any effort.

The trainee's communication skills, attitude, behaviour and feelings during the exercise should form the basis for self-appraisal and feedback from the trainer. From this feedback, the trainee should learn which words, behaviour and approach to pupils are most appropriate for the circumstances.

Role play can provide a mirror in which participants can see themselves as others see them. This should encourage insight into their own behaviour and sensitivity towards others' opinions, attitudes and needs. The benefits of changes in these aspects can be readily demonstrated, thereby bringing about any desired modifications.

The benefits of role play as a training tool are dependent on three things:

- the design of the exercise;
- the quality of the feedback; and
- control of the trainer.

Design

The design of each exercise should be governed by the requirements of the overall training objectives. Three factors need to be considered:

- *Credibility* – the degree to which the situation may be identified by the trainee as one that is likely to be encountered in real life.

- *Relevance* – the scenario must allow the trainer to cover all the desired learning points.

- *Complexity* – the level of complexity must not overwhelm the trainee, but should take into account current knowledge, understanding and ability.

Feedback

This must be constructive, otherwise it will become counterproductive, sap confidence and erect barriers to learning. Positive feedback can reinforce effective behaviour, instil confidence and highlight specific areas for improvement in a way that should be acceptable by the trainee.

Control

To get the best out of any role-play exercise, the trainer must maintain overall control in situations where it is difficult to predict what may happen. If situations arise that are not going to be helpful to the trainee, the trainer must be ready to intervene. This is particularly important if any danger or damage is likely to be involved to the participants of the exercise, to any other road user, or to property.

To get the best results from the role-play exercise, the trainer needs to be:

- Pro-active – to questions that will test the trainee's knowledge, ability, attitude and understanding; as the session develops, opportunities should be taken to prompt the trainee's response and test flexibility.

- Reactive – to do exactly as told, acting on the level of ability, and character being portrayed, responding well to any instruction given and following instructions to the letter – providing it is safe to do so.

When planning exercises, it is useful for trainers to understand how the SE uses role play for testing purposes during the Part 3 exam (covered earlier in this book).

The importance of staying in role

For any role-play exercise to be effective, both parties must stay 'in role'. Therefore anything that is said during the exercise should be said 'in role'.

However, particularly during the early stages of training, there may be situations where either the trainee is becoming more and more confused, or there is a threat of danger. In these situations, the trainer must take control, if necessary coming out of role. In such situations, in order to prevent the trainee from becoming even more confused, this departure from role must be made clear.

Once 'out of role', the trainer will need to use Q&A to discover whether or not the trainee understands why the exercise was interrupted. For example, the trainer could ask, 'Why do you think I've had to come out of role?' Depending on the circumstances, and the trainee's response to the questions, the situation may need to be recreated to give a second opportunity for positive learning to take place.

If a trainee is really struggling, a demonstration may be useful with the roles being reversed by the trainer taking on the role of the instructor.

In any circumstances, there must be no doubt in the mind of either party as to whether they are 'in role' or 'out of role'.

SUMMARY

Whatever level of driving instruction you intend to become involved with, you should seek to continually develop your practical teaching skills – whether this be on a personal or a professional basis. We hope that this book helps you to achieve these aims.

John Miller, Tony Scriven, Margaret Stacey

Index

The Driving Instructor's Handbook
Twelfth Edition
John Miller, Tony Scriven & Margaret Stacey

'The Driving Instructor's Handbook *is recommended
by the Driving Standards Agency for those studying for
the Approved Driving Instructor's qualifying examination.'*
Driving Standards Agency Register of Approved
Driving Instructors

'*An up-to-date copy of* The Driving Instructor's
Handbook *is as essential for a fully qualified instructor
as it is for those seeking to pass the ADI qualifying examinations.'*
John Lepine MBE, General Manager, The Motor Schools Association

'*...excellent reading for those in the business of instructors training.'*
Driving Magazine

The fact that *The Driving Instructor's Handbook* is now in its 12th edition
underlines its importance within the driving instructor training industry. It
retains its status as a bestseller and is not only recommended to trainee instructors, but also used as an authoritative guide for experienced ADIs.

The driver training and testing industry has undergone dramatic changes over
the past few years to ensure that new drivers are better able to cope with the
ever-increasing demands made on them. The authors update the Handbook
regularly, which ensures that all relevant information is made readily available.

Highly readable and practical, the Handbook includes comprehensive guidance
on:

- the role of the driving instructor;
- the ADI register and qualifying examination, and preparing for it;
- the responsibilities of the driver;
- the car – a chapter on basic mechanical principles;
- driving – an explanation of safe driving techniques;
- driver training – including the teaching of people with disabilities;
- the L driving test – theory and practice;
- driving lorries, buses and motorcycles.

The Driving Instructor's Handbook is essential reading for all those involved in
the training of drivers and instructors at all levels.

£19.95   ISBN 0 7494 3830 4

Learn to Drive: In 10 easy stages
Third Edition
Margaret Stacey
Illustrated by Andy Rice

'Quite simply, this is the best book for learner drivers I have read.'

Kenneth Parker, ADI

'The best driver teaching aid I have encountered.'

Andy Howes, ADI

'Comprehensive and sensibly structured, guides the learner step-by-step through every essential aspect of driver training. I would not be without it.'

Ken Dove, ADI

About to take your driving test? How confident are you of passing first time? As with any examination, your success depends very much on how well prepared you are.

Learn to Drive in 10 Easy Stages is now established as one of the most popular and best-selling guides to preparing for your driving test. By following the carefully structured step-by-step programme, it is guaranteed to boost your confidence and double your chances of passing first time.

This edition of *Learn to Drive* has been fully revised and updated to take account of the new test format. Designed to be as user friendly as possible, this clearly illustrated guide will teach you all you need to ensure that you are well prepared for the theory and practical tests. It covers:

- getting to know the car;
- the first steps in learning to drive;
- handling all the manoeuvres;
- using common sense and avoiding danger;
- coping with higher speeds;
- dealing with difficult situations.

For half the cost of a driving lesson, you can immediately improve your chances of success. Join the many thousands of people who have passed first time with the help of *Learn to Drive in 10 Easy Stages*!

£8.99

ISBN: 0-7494-3019-2

The Advanced Driver's Handbook
Second Edition
Margaret Stacey
Illustrated by Andy Rice

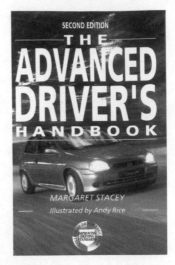

When does the learning process faced by every driver end? For many, the acquisition of a UK Driver's Licence is seen as the conclusion of this process. However, as road casualty figures testify, this common assumption is wrong; learning is an ongoing process. Whether newly qualified or experienced, all drivers should be aware of the need to improve their skills to ensure greater safety for themselves and others.

Fully revised and updated, this new edition of *The Advanced Driver's Handbook* is a practical guide to improving your abilities. Combining established advanced driving skills with defensive techniques, the book provides a clear insight into:

- understanding what causes road accidents – and knowing how to avoid them;
- the use of high performance handling techniques which increase stability and improve car control skills;
- hazard awareness and anticipation.

Packed with clear illustrations to make the task of becoming an advanced driver easier, this new edition also gives detailed information on advanced driver training and tests offered by organisations such as IAM, RoSPA and CODE. Easy-to-follow and rich in practical guidance, *The Advanced Driver's Handbook* is essential reading for any driver wanting to develop his or her skills.

£8.99

ISBN 0-7494-1501-0